Get Rich Slowly
Invest in Real Estate

Luis A. Belmonte

Illustrations by Scott H. Miller

First published in 2013 by Luis Belmonte as a paperback original. Also available as an ebook on Smashwords.com.

Copyright © 2013 by Luis A. Belmonte

All rights reserved. No part of this publication may be reproduced or transmitted in any form without written permission from the author.

ISBN: 978-0-615-75755-1

Cartoons copyright © 2013 by Scott H. Miller

Cover design © 2013 by Terri Driscoll at Driscoll Design

Contents

Introduction..................................4

1. A Bit of Investment Advice.......................6
2. Do You Belong in the Real Estate Business?
....15
3. Leverage and Inflation.....................23
4. How Do You Buy Right?....................33
5. So You Want to Be a Developer!...........43
6. A Short Course in Negotiations.............69
7. The Fine Art of Selling.......................79
8. Lease Documents, Tenant Improvements, Evictions and Bankruptcy........................92
9. Real Estate Investment Trusts..............102
10. Entitlements................................112
11. Land..119
12. Single Family..............................125
13. Apartments.................................130
14. Office Space................................139
15. Retail.......................................146
16. Industrial...................................153
17. Grab Bag...................................161
18. Corporate Culture..........................163

Introduction

A famous man once said: "Some men learn by listening; a few learn from reading; but most men have to go ahead and pee on the electric fence." I've peed on a few electric fences and you may be able to avoid a similar fate by reading what follows.

That was a learning experience I won't forget.

I started in the real estate business in 1956 helping my father with his rental houses. Except for a small interlude in Vietnam, I've been at it ever since. I know little or nothing about single-family subdivisions, regional malls, hotels, trailer parks (excuse me, *mobile home communities*, I get to call them trailer parks because I lived in one after WWII), or resort properties. I've built, rehabilitated financed, leased, demolished and managed property of all types except those five. It's been a good life, and I wouldn't trade it for the career of anybody I know. Over the course of all those years, I've distilled a few lessons that might be useful to you. Before I go soft in the head, I thought I'd pass them along.

A good friend of mine has a rule I try to follow. If you are going to express a controversial opinion, especially a political opinion (of which I have many), it's a good idea to preface the statement with the phrase "in my opinion." Tends to keep the ego in check.

This literary effort is designed to be interactive. Some of you who read it will know more about real estate than I do. Many of you will know more about certain aspects of the business than I do. Feel free to correct my ignorance. I will be happy to make corrections, with attribution (unless you ask for anonymity). The address is lbelmonte@7hp. Seven Hills Properties is the name chosen by my business partner and myself. What else would two WOPs (an ethnic slur that originally meant "without papers") call their company? For those of you deficient in Italian and/or geography, it's the seven hills of Rome. Some of you may find the term WOP offensive. I don't. I'm glad that my grandparents had the courage to get on a boat and come to the land of opportunity, where those who got here earlier (English, German, African, Irish, Chinese, and the Asians who walked across the Aleutians about 25,000 years ago) held them in contempt. Contempt didn't seem to do them any harm. It probably provided additional motivation to succeed.

1. A Bit of Investment Advice

Why Bother?

In order to live a good, long life in the USA, you need to make some serious money. Average life expectancy in this country, as of the end of 2011, was 78 years. It has been increasing at the rate of 3 months per year since 1900. There is clearly an upper limit to the life span of human beings (barring some major scientific breakthrough), but we aren't yet at the limit. You will not have enough money to support yourself in your old age unless you have an investment program. Odds on the lottery are very long. Unless your employer floats an Initial Public Offering (where shares of stock in a company are sold to the general public--another form of lottery), and you're included, working for wages won't get you serious money. We all tend to spend what we earn (and then some). CEOs, celebrities and professional athletes make serious money (usually for relatively short periods of time), but, if you're one of those, you probably aren't reading this book. In any event, your odds of making the NBA are about the same as the lottery, maybe longer. Social Security is not going to be around much longer in its present form. Even in its current form, relatively high earners end up with almost nothing after taxes and Medicare deductions. The 401k is a great program. The ability to save without being taxed (until withdrawal) gives you a chance to put away semi-serious money. Invest every dime you can; and get every cent of your employer match. It's still not enough. You need more than you are making to have a comfortable retirement. Travel costs money, and you will need a lot more medical care (most of which the government will not be paying for, because Medicare is even broker than Social Security). Real estate is one vehicle for generating a reliable source of income for your "golden" years. (They are only "golden" if you equate loss of hearing and eyesight, sagging muscles, thin skin, increased levels of anxiety, and getting up to pee several times a night with precious metal.)

Diversification?

Standard investment advice is that you should have a diversified portfolio of stocks, bonds, real assets, commodities, etc. Several Nobel Prizes have been awarded for that advice, if recollection serves. If it was ever good advice, it is no longer. A very wealthy friend of mine said of his portfolio in 2008, "I was perfectly diversified, and I watched it all go down together." Markets worldwide are far too closely correlated to rely on diversification as a safe haven. Some of your money should be kept in that fashion. I also think every portfolio ought to have some short positions as additional insurance (sale of a borrowed security, commodity or currency with the expectation that the asset will fall in value). However, a significant portion of your investments should be concentrated in something that you study carefully. A plethora of investment information is available, but most of it is impenetrable. Lots of very smart people spend lots of brainpower smoking the numbers. I've sat in numerous corporate meetings watching red turn to green right before my eyes. The only way to get through the smoke and mirrors is to know a whole lot about a little piece of the economy. Real estate is a good little piece, because there are fewer moving parts, and the really smart folks don't bother with it for the most part (meaning that there is less smoke and fewer mirrors). Real estate investment can also be subdivided into bite-sized increments, which you can master in detail. In general, you should take a significant piece of your savings to invest in something that interests you and you should spend time becoming an expert on that asset class--oil wells, commodities, a selected industry, whatever. If you really know an asset class, you will know when to get in and get out. And, no matter what the stock jockeys tell you, buy and hold is a fools' game. There is a time to hold 'em and a time to fold 'em in every investment known to the human species. There will always be investment manias and misallocation, because the markets are made up of human beings, who are herd animals.

What is an Investment?

I got my first car in 1956, when I was 16. It was a 1950 Plymouth. For those of you too young to remember, Chrysler Corporation used to make Plymouth. It was their Chevy class car. It cost $300 (probably $4,000 in today's dollars). My standard practice was to buy a dollar's worth of gas, which was about four gallons in those days. One day, I came home and proudly announced that I'd bought a whole tank of gas. My father's response was: "Depends what you'd rather have than money." I've tried to bring that thought to mind when I am buying something or investing.

My mother used to "invest" in expensive shoes. When she got old, her feet got bigger and she couldn't wear them. She died flat broke. If you want to piss away money on fancy shoes, go for it. Just don't get it confused with investing.

I have a little mental construct that you might find useful. I divide all things (aside from consumables) on which we spend money into three categories—investments, collectables and toys. And further divide into real property and personal property.

I have a dozen of these old valuable tennis sweaters.

In personal property, stocks and bonds are investments. A stock is theoretically the present value of future earnings. In the long enough run, that's probably true. A bond is a loan you make. At the end of the term, you get your principal back and get a fixed rate of interest in the interim. Oriental rugs and diamonds are collectables.

Unless you are a dealer, you buy retail and sell wholesale. Typically, you buy when you're flush (when everybody else is buying) and sell when you need the money (when everybody else is selling). Not a recipe for enrichment. If you are an astute buyer, you might keep up with inflation and make a few bucks. A luxury car of any kind is a toy. After you've driven it five miles, it's worth considerably less than you paid for it, and the value goes down every day thereafter. Until it becomes an antique, at which point it's a collectable.

In real property, an apartment building is an investment. It has an income stream, the capitalized value of which can be easily calculated. Capitalization rates change somewhat over time, but you can always sell the income stream for the current cap rate. A house is a collectable. Lots of folks got confused about that in the mid-2000s. Aside from periods of frenzy, which come along occasionally, a house is worth reproduction cost, less deferred maintenance. Value can be added if the neighborhood upgrades, or value can be lost if a neighborhood degrades, but most house price appreciation is simply a reflection of inflation (which increases nominal replacement cost). Vacation property is a toy. When times are tough, it has no value at all.

An important ancillary take-away from this discussion is the knowledge that your house IS NOT an investment. It is shelter from the storm, a place to raise your family, a psychological anchor, a vehicle to express your taste, one of the bigger financial commitments you are liable to make in your lifetime, but it is not an investment. It can be a savings program. If you buy a suitable house in a good neighborhood and maintain it, you can sell it when you need the money for what you paid for it plus inflation, maybe a little more. If you got a fixed rate, amortizing loan (a wonderful middle class boondoggle brought to you by financially illiterate politicians—a good deal for the borrower, a bad deal for the taxpayer), you have a savings program with a tax break at the end ($500,000 gain tax free). In any event, don't confuse owning a house with investing in real estate.

Some Investment Basics

In terms of thinking about investment return, it is vital to think in real dollars, not nominal dollars. Two examples help illustrate. Since I did my first deal in 1967, the dollar has lost about 90% of its value. My target in buying several beat up Victorian flats in San Francisco in those days was to pay $15,000 per unit. Those units today are worth about $500,000. Some of the increase in value is due to the insanity of rent control, and some is due to the hellish process that passes for entitlement in San Francisco, both of which have constricted the supply of new buildings, but the rest is inflation. Bear in mind, $150 to $500 in 45 years sounds a lot less impressive than $15 to $500. Another shining example the effects of is the Alternate Minimum Tax. It was originally passed to ensnare 300 or so high-income folks who were paying no federal income tax. Mostly widows who were fully invested in muni bonds. Of course, they had paid taxes by buying an investment whose return was about 2/3 of taxable bonds, because the whole underpinning of the muni market is a subsidy to allow local governments to borrow at a cheaper rate by making the interest income tax free. Such subtleties are easily lost in the fog of political combat. Pandering trumps sound economic policy almost every time. AMT now impacts literally millions of tax returns and has to be "patched" every year to avoid a public outcry, simply because it was not indexed. What was rich at inception is now merely upper middle class.

When investing in real estate, it is important to know that value is all about the income stream. After discounting the income stream for inflation, the only increase in value can come from speculative frenzy, population increase, or increase in the flow of money.

When you see a frenzy (prices unhooked from spendable cash flow), get out of the way. Bubbles are not that hard to spot. When prices become disconnected from the historic norm; when the price doesn't make any sense unless the exit is to the next fool in the daisy chain; when you hear "it's different this time" get into the next county. If you are sophisticated enough, short the market. Just remember to design a short with a long time frame. Markets can often stay stupid for a long time.

When population increases, real estate prices go up because more people means more demand for a place to live and a place to shop and a place to work. The level of increase will depend upon geography. Where it's easy to build, there is less appreciation of existing real estate. So, you need to look for mountains (which are hard to build on due to infrastructure and structural costs) and water. The other form of geography is political geography. Every time a tree gets hugged, real estate investors make money. Political geography is less reliable than physical geography because the mountains tend to fade away when the economy goes in the toilet. We'll discuss the entitlement swamp in a later chapter (at length).

Does this mean that you can't make money buying real estate in places that are losing population? No. But you aren't going to get any appreciation. You might not even get your original capital back. So, you have to buy at a price such that the cash flow over the holding period provides a satisfactory return. Think of it as if you owned a building sitting on leased land. At the end of the lease term, you own nothing.

The flow of money also creates appreciation. The great secret that most politicians don't know (or choose to ignore) is that money has legs. It goes where it thinks it can get the best risk-adjusted return. That was always true, but used to require some sneaking around. In today's economy, money can be moved with a computer in a heartbeat. If you want to figure out where prosperity is happening, follow the money. The prices of coops in NYC and lavish houses in Los Altos Hills can be directly related to Wall Street bonuses and IPO proceeds respectively. Latin America has always been poorer than it should be because many people who make spare money take it to Miami or Houston (because they fear that their government will steal from them). More money means the existing population wants more square feet in which to live, and more (and more upscale) places to shop. Work areas become more spacious and more opulent. More warehouses are required to store more and better goods.

Rates of Return

As the title of this masterwork implies, I do not think real estate is a get-rich-quick endeavor. There are lots of courses (with DVDs available after) being offered in windowless hotel conference rooms testifying to the contrary. However, all get rich schemes have nothing to do with real estate, whether peddled in the aforementioned monuments to poor décor, or glass walled conference rooms high above Wall Street. All such schemes, at whatever level of sophistication, are about leverage. We will discuss the merits of leverage later, but high levels of leverage are simply another lottery play (you are betting you can roll the debt, or that appreciation will save your ass, or that you can sell to the greater fool before the market corrects). Real estate that is levered to a reasonable level will, over the long haul, produce returns somewhere between stocks and bonds. The top 25 or 30% is equity and should perform like a stock; the bottom 70 or 75% performs like a bond.

And I'd like to buy that bridge you have for sale, too.

2. Do You Belong in the Real Estate Business?

Instinct

Many years ago, I worked for a national development company as a rookie developer. I was sent to Fresno to source a site for an industrial building. I came back to the home office with a site I liked a lot. My boss asked me where my site was in relationship to the sites on which the Trammell Crow Company (our big dog competitor) was building. Since my site was a long way from the Crow sites, he questioned my judgment. Being the stubborn turkey I am, I was insistent that I had a better location for an industrial building and that the Crow guy was simply taking the path of least resistance by building on the periphery. In order to convince the boss, I chartered a small plane and we flew to Fresno (he was too impatient to drive and I didn't have the endurance for eight hours in the car with him). When the plane was about five miles from the west edge of town, he pointed to my site and said something like, "is that it?" When I responded in the affirmative, he was more than satisfied. The dirt in question was next to the main rail line, close to a freeway interchange, had an adequate depth, the right size for a building in that market, etc. He got all that in one glance from five miles away because he had great real estate instincts.

You are not going to make money in the real estate business unless you can develop good instincts for what will work and what won't. In the case of the Fresno building, we didn't make much money, because Fresno is a flat spot. Too easy to build; very little rent growth. But we covered the downside, because we had one of the best located and configured buildings in town, and it was easily divisible into increments that worked in that market. We kept it full and sold it for a decent profit. There is nothing wrong with that outcome.

Doing deals and running property is not for everybody. If the thought of chasing a deadbeat tenant, or mud wrestling with a lender, or unplugging a toilet grosses you out, find a more civilized way to make a living. In order to get good, you are going to have to rub your nose in the business until you have a really good feel for what will work and what won't. And that's true even if the closest you get to the bricks and sticks at the peak of your career is a conference room high above Midtown Manhattan. If you don't understand the practicalities of property leasing and operation, you will make dumb decisions.

I am a big believer in psychological testing. Not that any individual test is a panacea. But taking a number of them will give you a good view of your personality. You should do this testing as a part of career planning or career changing.

The first reason to take the tests is to get a truer picture of yourself. We all think we know who we are. The vast majority of us are full of bullshit. Our own picture of who we are and the truth about who we are have hardly been in the same room. If you don't believe me, find somebody you know reasonably well, who is somewhat different than you, and ask him for a thumbnail description of your personality. The results will startle you.

The second reason is to bring home in a stark fashion that there are lots of kinds of personalities, of which you are just one. You need to treat different people differently. Other people's hot buttons are not the same as yours. If you are building a project, you will need to deal with a land owner, bureaucrats, politicians, lenders, contractors, neighbors and tenants. Vastly different approaches are required for dealing with each of those constituencies. If you understand your own personality, and understand that the people you are dealing with have personalities, you stand a much better chance of

Finally, the process of personality testing may avoid what the shrinks call cloning. People asso people they like. Why do you like someone?

Similarity: You like people who are like you

Familiarity: Absence does not make the heart grow fonder. The more you see somebody you like, the greater are the chances that affection will increase. That's why the sale is made on the fifth (or sixth) call. By then, the prospect is familiar with the salesperson

Association: You like people who know the people you like, and went to the same school you did, and enjoy the same movies you do, and belong to the same organizations

Appearance: It ain't fair, but good looking people tend to be better liked than ugly people. If you don't think that's true, consider the amount of money spent on clothing, gyms, cosmetics, beauty parlors, cosmetic surgery, etc.

Praise: Shameless flattery works almost every time in almost every situation. If I tell you that you are really smart and really pretty, you tend to think well of me. Praise is the most powerful weapon on earth.

When you hire a staff or build a development team, the natural tendency will be to hire people you like. Big mistake! You end up with people like you, which means you will engage in group think, and exacerbate both your strengths and weaknesses. You should be looking to build your team around people with skills different than your own. Finding unfortunate looking people (except for the sales force) who don't blow smoke up your ass, and come from very different backgrounds, will make you money.

I am especially fond of aptitude tests. Again, take a bunch of them. You will see a pattern develop. Most people go through life trying to find a satisfactory career through experimentation. They take a job just to put food on the table. They hate the job. Take another job, and another, until they find something that works or they get so far in debt that they have to keep going to the same job to pay the bills (and dream of vacations and retirement). I am not asking you to find your passion or the color of your parachute. I am saying you can more efficiently find an acceptable way to make a living with the help of the tests.

Human beings seem to have a hierarchy of needs—water, food, sex, shelter (at a certain age, shelter trumps sex), security, wealth, etc. Somewhere high on the list is job satisfaction. The work you do gives you a sense of self-worth. You feel good about selling a house or writing a brief or designing a building. If you have a job that provides that reward, it's a lot easier to get up every weekday morning and go to work.

No job or profession is going to be perfect. That's why it's called work. There is routine and drudgery and ugly aspects to almost any endeavor. You may wish to be a painter, but you also have to get the stuff sold in order to eat. You may lust to be the CEO, but you have to deal with your board and the press and Wall Street analysts. The objective is to find something to do that is mostly satisfactory and then shape the situation to better comport with your skill set. Work your strengths and finesse your weaknesses (by teaming up with people whose strengths are your weaknesses).

Personality and Real Estate

Different aspects of the real estate business work for different sorts of people. As you approach the business, you should figure out where you want to end up.

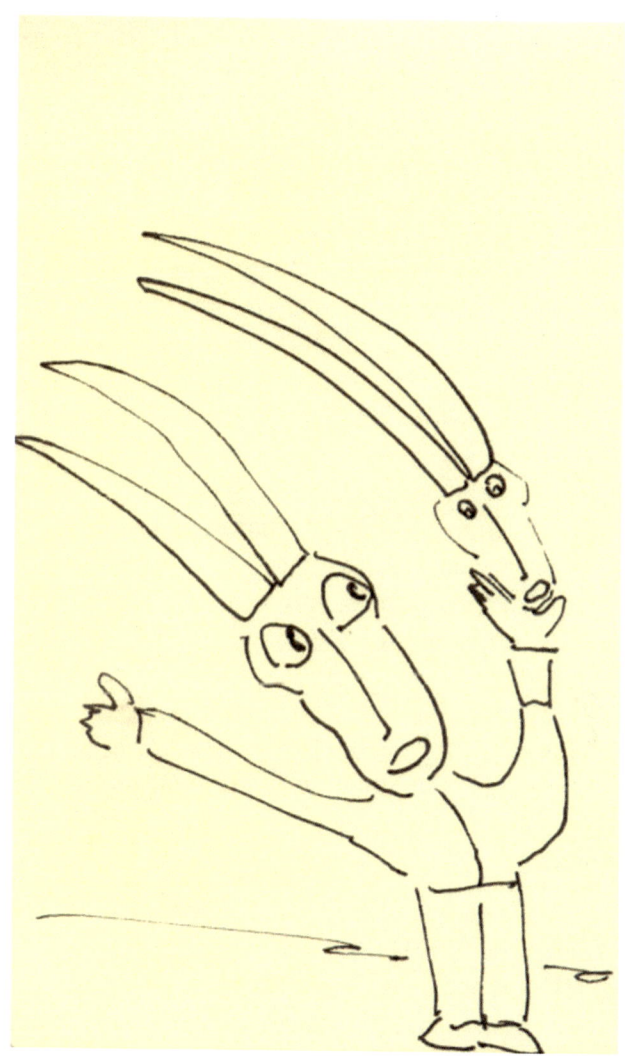

It turns out I'm pretty much who I thought I was.

Architects are our artists. They are inductive thinkers, creative types. In addition, great architects are excellent politicians who exude professional/artistic aura, which gets their ideas past planning commissions. Quite often, architects decide that they can develop and finance their own ideas. This is almost invariably a disaster. The skill set required to get a deal financed and built is not often in the same wheelhouse as creativity and political charisma.

Property managers have a high sense of responsibility, as the shrinks define that term. Like nurses, social workers, and public safety workers, they think they can make a difference. A good property manager really cares about the welfare of his/her tenants. When asking "how's the wife and kids," they mean it. At one point in my life, I had to hire and supervise property managers all around the world. My way of judging their suitability after they had been with us awhile was to accompany the manager on a visit to one or more tenants, and watch the body language between the tenant and the manager. If the tenant liked the manager, I was happy. Many property owners, most notably institutional owners, judge managers by the efficiency and thoroughness of their reporting, as opposed to their relationship with the tenants. That's one of the reasons I love competing with institutional owners. Some tenants move at the end of the lease term because they need more or less space. Some go broke. Many of the remainder who move do so because they hate the owner, usually in the form of its representative.

The successful providers of debt and equity are analysts. They are deductive thinkers who do rigorous analysis that is entirely fact based. At least they pretend that it is entirely fact based. Lots of analysis is ex post facto rationalization by those doing what they want to do with people they want to do it with. However, the best lenders and investors are pretty damn rigorous. The only way to approach them successfully is with a well marshaled, fact based case.

Sales people are born, not made. They deal in emotional currency. They can spot buying signals. They have an instinct for feelings of fear and greed. They know how to find the hot buttons and push them repeatedly. Once the ink is on the line, they know how to reinforce the decision (so that buyer's remorse does not set in) by telling their principal (repeatedly) how wise the decision to buy or sell or rent really was. In psychological terms, salespeople are highly socialized. They want to follow the rules. That is why there are quotas and territories and contests. They crave recognition for following the rules, which is why there are cruises for the top producers and pictures in the local business rag. The fastest way to a salesperson's heart is to tell him/her how much you value their help (as opposed to the rejection and scorn they deal with all day every day); pay them promptly when the ink is on the paper; and buy a tombstone announcing the deal with their name in big letters (and your name in small letters). I seldom do a deal of any kind without sales help. I am no good at emotional communication. I need a translator. What is the hot button of the other team? What did they like and not like about my presentation? I can't answer those questions accurately. A good salesperson can.

Developers are the system's gangsters. A modicum of creativity is required to see the deal that others don't see (or figure out which of the competitors to imitate, or which architect to hire). But the key personality ingredient is low socialization. Nobody likes a developer. Nobody wants change. If you care about what others think, find another way to make a living. The most common word a developer hears is "NO!" The seller of the land wants more than you can afford to pay; the neighbors hate your project (they're using the vacant land as a park); the planners want a fee you can't afford; the politicians won't play unless you contribute; the lender wants to lend less than you need, and take your first born as collateral; and the tenant wants a year's free rent while you are making debt service and paying taxes.

I've never gotten the right information to give you a good psychological sketch of contractors, but I do have a few hints. I can't tell what a building will look like from a set of plans. I have to go kick the wall of a similar building. The rendering helps some, but the plans and specs do nothing for my comprehension. A good builder can absolutely visualize the finished product when looking at plans. Another common characteristic is the urge to draw. On numerous occasions when walking a job under construction, I will ask a question which is answered by the contractor or tradesman picking up a scrap of lumber and drawing me a picture.

You should do some thinking about your personality type and skill set before setting out to make a career in the real estate business, and you should also figure out the niche into which you most comfortably fit. That does not mean you can disappear into the niche. In order to be a professional in any of the related fields, you need to know something about demographics, construction, finance, selling, politics, land use law, etc. As an entree into the field, you can come at it from any direction. The purpose of personality analysis is to try to steer your career in a direction that will produce a high level of job satisfaction at the end. I did my first sale transaction in 1963 and my first development deal in 1968. I have been at it ever since. In my declining years, I do it as a hobby (because my golf sucks and I'm too impatient to fish). Doing deals for the joy of doing it is the greatest career blessing I can imagine.

3. Leverage and Inflation

What's Leverage Got to do With It?

Real Estate is a capital-intensive business. With the exception of some pension funds deals, almost all investments involve some borrowed money. This borrowed money, also called leverage, can magnify returns (thus, the get-rich-quick schemes). It can also magnify loss. If you are leveraged 9 to 1, and the value of your investment goes down 10%, you are fully broke. Ask Lehman Brothers and Bear Stearns (who were leveraged about 40 to 1 in 2008) how that works. There is a rational way to use leverage, especially if you can get fixed rate debt. I cannot imagine why any lender would want to issue long term, fixed rate debt in a world without a gold standard to anchor the value of the currency, but they do. As of this writing Fannie and Freddie (owned by you, the taxpayer) are writing lots of 30-year fixed-rate loans. Money is on sale!!

The first question to ask is whether the proposed leverage is positive or negative. Positive means that the rate of interest on the loan is equal to or less than the yield on the investment. If you can buy an investment that yields eight, and get a loan that costs seven, you're in tall clover. You want to be very careful of taking on leverage if the interest rate exceeds your cash yield. That is a recipe for a visit with the bankruptcy judge, unless you have a lot of equity in the deal. The constant (interest plus principal paydown) can exceed your yield, if you can live without immediate cash flow. In a situation where there is significant inflation on the horizon or the (very reasonable) prospect of rent increases in the near term, you can fudge a little and project positive leverage in the second or third year, but I wouldn't press it beyond that.

So how does leverage help you? I'll try to illustrate with a simplified example. Let's say you are buying a deal where rents can escalate as fast as inflation. Either an apartment building in a tight market with no rent control or a commercial deal with a long lease including annual rent increases in line with inflation. Let's say inflation is 3%. Let's say the deal yields 8% and you get an interest only 10-year loan at 8%. Let's say you put down 20% and the deal costs $100,000. We'll sell the deal in year 11. All of this is more facile than the real world and includes no transaction costs, but you'll get the basic idea.

Year/Cash flow on equity/Cash flow on debt/Value of building

1	$1,600	$0	$100,000
2	$1,648	$192	$103,000
3	$1,697	$390	$106,090
4	$1,748	$694	$109,927
5	$1,801	$803	$113,225
6	$1,854	$827	$116,622
7	$1,910	$852	$120,120
8	$1,967	$877	$123,724
9	$2,026	$903	$127,436
10	$2,077	$930	$131,259
11	$0	$0	$135,968

So, you sell the deal in the beginning of year eleven based on your latest rent increase for $136,000. You originally invested $20,000. You owe the lender $80,000, leaving you with $36,000. In addition, you got cash flow of $18,300 on your original investment and cash flow of $6,500 because the yield from the property became greater than the interest on the debt due to inflationary increases in rent. You put 20 in and got 81 back after 10 years. Not too bad. Inflation and leverage were your friends. In order to do a fair calculation, you have to have to escalate the $20,000 by inflation to get your real dollar profit in current dollars, but I'll let you do that. You also have to account for the taxes you will pay on your profit (less the present value of tax savings during the period of ownership), to get a true return on your investment.

Some of you may have been expecting an Internal Rate of Return spread sheet, meaning the present value of all cash flow and sale proceeds. I prefer to think of IRRs as an intestinal disorder. I do the calculation to satisfy a lender, not as a decision-making vehicle. My view is that deals are done on an envelope. If it works on the envelope, the IRR will probably be OK. If it doesn't work on the envelope, and the IRR looks good, you better redo the IRR.

To get IRR in perspective, you can do it in your head by adding the going capitalization rate and your growth assumption. If you buy at a nine; assume rental growth of three; and sell at a nine, your IRR is 12. As a practical matter, you have turnover expenses that eat some of the cash flow, and your exit cap should be projected 100 basis points (a basis point is .01%) below your acquisition cap (because the building is 10 years older). Calculated correctly, an unleveraged IRR is usually 100 basis points higher than your acquisition cap rate. If you buy at a 9, your IRR will be 10. The leveraged IRR will obviously depend upon what kind of a loan you are able to get.

The problem with the worship of IRR is that the two most important moving parts (growth rate and exit cap) are total WAGs (wild ass guesses). The value of doing careful IRR analysis is that it is a good vehicle for comparing the relative attractiveness of similar investments (one B grade apartment building with another). If you are investing other peoples' money, it adds rigor to the process. It also creates the impression that you know what you are doing.

You are not going to get any fancy mathematical footwork from me. I'm a dumb developer. I'm not trying to maximize profit; I'm trying not to get slaughtered in a falling market. Dealing with a rising market is not a problem. A gorilla can make money in a rising market.

I am reminded of one of my anchor principles. John Kenneth Galbraith was a highly regarded economist when I was young. He taught at Harvard and Princeton and wrote a lot of books. He was the pet economist of the Kennedy family. Most of what he wrote, in my opinion, was socialist claptrap. He did write one thing (maybe he stole it from somebody else) that has animated my thinking ever since I read it. He defined financial genius as a short memory in a rising market.

We're fine unless the winds of change come up.

Can you depend on inflation?

Based on my reading of history, I believe that inflation will always be with us. There is little if any chance that we will ever again peg the value of paper currency to gold or any other hard peg. That means that paper currency is just that: paper. Politicians are good at spending money. It theoretically solves problems. It buys votes. It feels good to take money from those who have and give it to those who don't. Politicians are not good at curbing spending. The growth of the State is almost inexorable. At some point, the ability to borrow is constrained by the unwillingness of anyone to lend. At that point, devaluation is by far the easiest path. The demise of the Roman Empire and the French Revolution can be traced directly to currency devaluation. The Romans added base metal to the coins and shaved them. Inflation has been going on for a long time. When I was a young man traveling in Europe, the French had just introduced the New Franc (worth 20 cents American). It was new because it was replacing an Old Franc, worth 2 cents American. The Lira exchange was 1,400 to the dollar.

Certainly, there are periods of deflation. After the passage of the Tax Act of 1986, real estate deflated, because we were all in the business of generating write-offs for investors who refused to give the government 70% of their ordinary income. When the top marginal rate went to 28% and a firewall was built between investment losses and ordinary income, all investment real estate was suddenly worth about 20% less. All of us were broke, whether we ended up in bankruptcy court (which many did) or not. The US and Europe went thru a deflation in the 30s. That was due to a contraction of the money supply, disappearance of credit, and a trade war.

In an era of paper currency, inflation will be the rule, not the exception. Even the most upright central banker is aiming for an inflation rate of 2%. For reasons that escape me, the economist establishment seems to think that a little inflation makes for greater economic growth. As long as you evaluate your investments using real (inflation adjusted) dollars (after tax), you will prosper. If you can get fixed rate leverage in an inflationary world, your returns will be magnified.

Ask a balloon maker if you want to hear about the upside of inflation.

How Much Should I Borrow (If I Can Find a Willing Lender)?

The answer depends on who you are and how much money you have and how much risk you are willing to tolerate.

Real estate is a capital-intensive business. Very few players (except pension funds) can operate all cash. Even if you could buy a significant asset for cash, it would probably not be wise to put that many eggs in one basket. So, you are going to use some leverage.

In my opinion, pension funds (a major source of funds for larger and more conservative transactions) should not use leverage at all. The object of a pension fund is to produce income for retirees. The investment plan should be fully diversified—stocks, bonds and real estate. Because many funds (especially the public employee variety) have unrealistic return goals, they are stretching into private equity, hedge funds, opportunistic real estate, etc., to get higher returns. Bad idea! Chasing high return involves high risk. The income security of retirees should not depend on high-risk bets. Since a mortgage (or note and deed) at a level up to 75 or 80 percent of value is the moral equivalent of a bond, a pension fund using leverage in a real estate deal is on both sides of the deal. Let the bond department deal in bonds. Real estate should be bought for cash flow (and, hopefully) an increase in inflation adjusted value based on increases in cash flow. Astute acquisition in the path of population growth or increasing flow of capital can enhance value creation.

Pension funds get conned by Wall Street investment managers. The typical deal theoretically involves an "alignment of interest" whereby the manager contributes 20% (or so) of the capital to do so-called "value add" deals. The objective is to buy a broken property; fix it up; and sell for a profit. The defect can be in financing, timing, physical defects, vacancy, or other issues. The investor puts up 80% of the equity and pays a success fee to the manager based on the IRR the deal produces. So the manager lines up a deal which will cost $100 all in, for example, $70 purchase price on the wounded property and $30 to fix it up. He then gets a loan commitment for $80 and borrows $70 to close. Next he spends the remaining $10 of loan proceeds and his $4 equity contribution. Right at the end (to pay for the last of the tenant improvements for the new tenants and the transaction costs of the sale), he calls for the pension fund money. Probably, the deal is already committed for sale when the last of the pension fund money comes in the door. The deal sells for $140. So, the manager gets $12 back for $4 invested. The pension fund gets $48 back for $16 invested... LESS an incentive fee paid to the manager because the IRR is huge (since the money was invested for only a few weeks or months). The manager gets a supercharged return and the pension fund has accomplished very little in terms of long term deployment to money to meet the needs of the retirees. Call me cynical, but I've looked at a lot of deals that look a lot like the one I've described (except a lot more zeros were involved).

If you're buying a well maintained apartment complex in a dense market in an urban area with a growing population, reasonable barriers to new construction and a decent supply/demand balance, 80% leverage is reasonable. The chances that rents will fall so far and vacancy will increase so much that you can't make debt service are very slim. Apartments will always rent in a dense market at a price. You just have to project how much that price might deteriorate based on past downturns in that market. If your debt service does not exceed your cash flow (with some reasonable room to spare) in the downside scenario, you're safe.

At the other end of the spectrum, if you are buying an office building in a tertiary market, where there are few barriers to entry, 50% leverage might be dangerous. In that instance, you need to be prepared for major rent decreases and very high vacancy. You should probably reserve a year's worth of debt service, and enough money to pay for tenant improvement upgrades to the whole building.

All of this assumes that you can get a rate of interest that is equal to or below the free and clear yield on the asset. If you are buying a deal at a 7 cap and borrowing at 9, it will take a whole lot of inflation to bail you out. Not a very good bet. If you are buying well below replacement cost and at the bottom of the cycle (meaning that rent increases can reasonably be projected), you can push this rule a little, but not too much. Also, remember that you can't compare the price you are paying to the cost of a new building. You have to take the cost of your building and add an amount that it would take to render your building equal in appeal to a new building (usually 10-20%) before deciding you bought below replacement cost.

4. How Do You Buy Right?

What is an Appropriate Investment Return?

Any investment should be judged on the risk related rate of return. Start with the perfectly safe investment. You sleep soundly all night with no dreams. That's technically referred to at the risk free rate. My simple mind calls that 3%. Recollection is that the exact number is 2.72, but I'll let you MBAs handle the filling in of that blank.

In order to get 3% in real dollars, you have to get compensated for inflation. Picking the right inflation assumption for a long-term investment is obviously a crap shoot. Since about 1980, 3% had been a fairly good number. The central banks aim for 2%, but don't seem to be able to get there on a regular basis. That would lead you to an unleveraged 6% rate of return as a target.

In a sense, picking the right inflation rate is not all that important. If you are buying a real estate asset that will turn tenancy on a regular basis, you can adjust rents to keep pace. If you are buying an asset with a long lease that has no provision for increases to keep pace with inflation, it is a real problem. In any event, you need to pick a reasonable target for purposes of this analysis.

As an aside, I think there are several inflation rates. The so-called core inflation excludes food and fuel. That's a great measure if you don't eat, drive or heat your home, but it practically useless otherwise. The price of housing is calculated as rent equivalent. Therefore, the index did not reflect the huge run-up in home prices between 2000 and 2007. I also think there may be a class-based difference. If you live in an apartment and shop at WalMart, inflation has been very muted. Rents have started to increase in 2012, but increases have been almost non-existent in the 20 years prior. Rent increases have not even kept up with so-called core inflation. Manufactured goods, sourced from around the world, have actually declined in price, in both nominal and real terms. If, on the other hand, you are upper middle class, you live in a different world. The cost of many luxury goods and services has increased at a rapid rate. My index is the cost of a good hotel room in New York City. That has tripled in the last 20 years. A more universal measurement might be tuition as a top tier private college. Tuition, room and board at the college I attended was $2,000 in 1962; it's about $80,000 now.

Now that we have a risk-free, inflation-adjusted rate, how do we judge any given investment? The return should vary with the level of risk that the return will not be paid, and the amount of work required to get the return. The spectrum is from Treasuries to junk bonds in personal property, and from an AAA net leased building to an old building leased to local credit in a tertiary city.

So, at this point, we need to figure out the return premium you should demand for an investment that is illiquid, involves backed-up plumbing, and requires you to chase deadbeat tenants. My answer is that a B or better quality, multi-tenant asset centrally located in a major metropolitan area that is not dying due to out-migration of people and/or money, should have a yield premium of 3%. That translates to an unleveraged IRR of 9%. Remember that your IRR calculation must include realistic vacancy, realistic turnover and transaction costs, and a VERY realistic exit cap (at least 100 basis points above your acquisition cap).

If you are buying a steel frame building on 5th Avenue in NYC, leased to an AAA tenant for 30 years, rent adjusting annually indexed to inflation of the New York MASA, the premium might be 50 basis points. At the other end of the spectrum, a tin shed rented month to month to a pool hall operator in Barstow probably rates at least 1,000 basis points of risk premium.

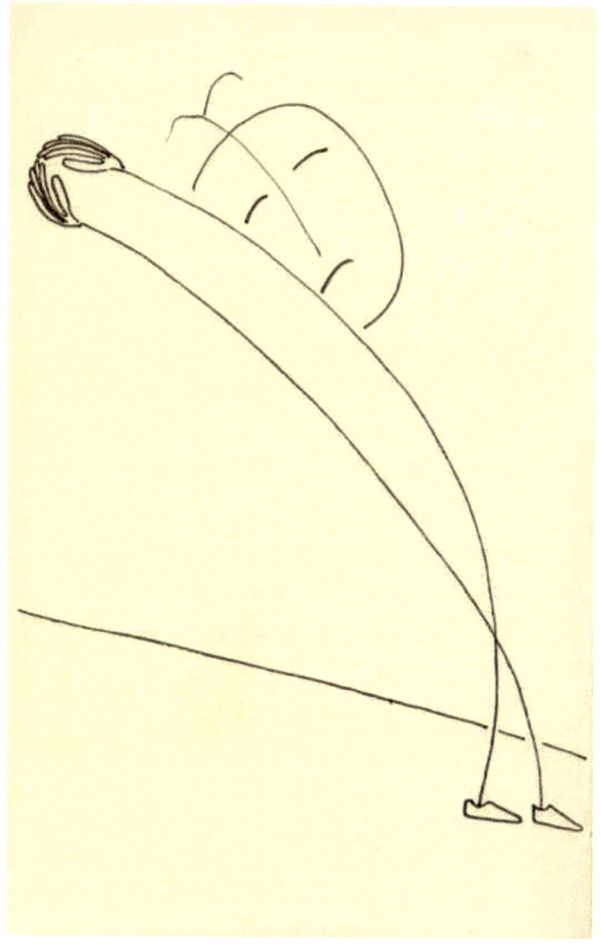

Bending over backward to reach for unrealistic investment returns.

The Property Pyramid

Here is another mental image that is helpful in looking at various real estate investments. It is common (or, at least it used to be when I was playing among the big dogs) to talk about the pyramid of property investments, as a way to distinguish the quality of an investment. The higher up the pyramid, the less the risk premium required for a sound investment.

At the very top are trophies and jewel boxes. Trophy properties are big and jewel boxes are small. Both are very high quality—very well located, timeless design, and high quality construction. Examples of trophies are the MetLife building in NYC, the Beverly Hills Hotel, and the Bank of America building in San Francisco. A jewel box would be a little office building in downtown Palo Alto or Bethesda. Those types of buildings will stay leased in almost any market, will attract institutional investors in almost any market and can be financed almost any time.

Down the pyramid, we come to institutional grade real estate. This is the stuff that pension funds will buy and insurance companies will finance. It includes all types of property in major markets (close in or central), fairly recent construction (or upgrade), which do not suffer from functional obsolescence.

The rest of the pyramid is everything else. You might get a loan from one of the few remaining S&Ls or a community bank. A lot of the paper is carried by sellers. Institutions won't get near it. It's your pool hall in Barstow. You can make money if you buy it right, and have a good pool hall operator/meth cooker, but you better get a good spread to the risk free rate, because there is minimum liquidity and you might have to carry a gun when you make the collection call.

One of the huge opportunities is the arbitrage available if you can translate a property from non-institutional to institutional. Arbitrage is taking advantage of a price difference between two or more markets: striking a combination of matching deals that capitalize upon the imbalance, the profit being the difference between the market prices. Sometimes, this is just a matter of timing. When the market gets hot, the line between the two tends to move down the pyramid. At one point in the late 90s, I listened to a presentation by a very big dog in the world of institutional investment talk about the deals she was making in mobile home parks. Usually, it requires some work. If you can find a property on the edge where some cosmetic work or a cure for functional obsolescence is possible, you can buy and sell at very different cap rates. Cap rate is short for capitalization rate, the rate of return on cost. If you invest $100 and get an annual return of $7, you've bought a deal at a 7 cap.

On many occasions, institutional buyers will pass on a property just because it is ugly. Getting a thick coat of lipstick on the pig can often do wonders to compress a cap rate. I once worked on an industrial deal that we bought for $3 million and sold about 15 years later for $100 million. In the meantime, we had torn down some of the buildings, built some new ones, and put in infrastructure. More important, we were in the path of progress. Silicon Valley moved in our direction, and the road in front of us was widened and highly improved. We went from being in a slum to being on the edge of a slum, with a good window onto a major thoroughfare. We carefully isolated the property from the surrounding area, had a lot of security, and had a big enough site to create a separate environment. The deal isn't quite as good as I make it sound. Our inflation adjusted cost basis was probably $50 million, but it was still a hell of a deal. And, just so you don't think too highly of me, I need to tell you that I was on the buying side, not the selling side, by the time the whole deal got done.

Out of this analysis come two opportunities and a warning. You can make money catching the movement of the line between institutional and non-institutional downward by selling into an institutional buying frenzy.

You can get a cap rate you wouldn't otherwise get when the big money comes your way. You can also make money by translating a non-institutional asset into an institutional asset by being in the path of an improving neighborhood or correcting functional or aesthetic defects. On the other hand, you can get slaughtered as an institutional buyer if an asset you bought when times were good gets into the Barstow pool hall status when sanity returns to the investment process. The usual solution, in that case, is to try to slip the dog into a package of otherwise decent deals, and pass it along to the next sucker.

Timing

A lot of people in the investment advice business are into "buy and hold." This strategy is combined with the instruction to average down if the stock you bought goes lower after you bought it. In other words, you should compound your error by doing more of the same. Or, as they say at the blackjack table—let's double up to catch up. It is a formula designed to have you on the Greyhound going home broke. That sort of advice used to be more popular among stock advisors before we went through a decade of no growth in stock prices. At all times, the advice is bunk. If you intend to be a holder of any type of asset, you need to buy when the price is right. If you buy at the top of the market, it's very hard to ever make any money, except with a very long hold (by which time inflation has masked your dumb decision). Remember, all investment performance needs to be judged in real dollars, after tax. In the old days (really old days) we used to have a concept called "spendable." That's the money you got to buy groceries after everybody else was paid. The concept of free and clear yield comes close, but "spendable" is a better concept.

All markets have cycles, because all markets involve transactions undertaken by human beings. If we were perfectly rational, there would be no manias. If information was perfectly distributed, and friction was eliminated from the deal process, there would never be an oversupply of product. However, we are partially rational beings dealing with imperfect information and lots of friction. Misallocation will always be with us! Human beings are herd animals who excel at rationalization.

It was a great time to sell.

Here's a little parable of the real estate market and its cycle. Some creative type (maybe an architect) gets an idea for a new product (a build-it-from-scratch-downtown--Santana Row in San Jose; mini storage-- invented by somebody in Texas in the 60s; the airfreight and rail hub --Alliance northwest of Dallas), or a variation on a product type, or an adaptive reuse (conversion of obsolete office to residential in downtown NYC). The first deal usually flops because the sponsor doesn't have the horsepower to pull it off, and nobody in the financing community is willing to take a chance on a novel product.

Then along comes some hard-eyed developer who has some pocket, and the confidence of some money players. He/she looks at the deal and says, "We tweak that a little, and cut out a few of the frills, and we can make it go." It's a huge success and soon there are imitators. If the developer has good sense, the deal gets sold before the field gets overcrowded.

At this point, the financial community gets in on the game. There are now comps (comparable rents and sale prices) to look at. Lenders like facts. Facts are all in the past. There are no future facts. Lenders want facts before they lend. Money is now available for the new product and we get a lot of it.

At the end of the cycle, we enter the "Lucky Irishman" phase. There's too much of the product in question; the pipeline is overflowing; but mine is prettier (or higher quality or better located or some other rationalization) and it will lease.

Now, comes the hour of the broker. There is a certificate for dinner for two at the best restaurant in town for any broker who shows the space, and a two year lease on a Porsche for anybody who gets a lease signed for X square feet or more.

Then, we start again. Some dreamer comes along with a scheme to alter the empty building in some fashion, or some hard ass figures out how to engineer the financing in such a way as to be able to rent for much less than the competitors. The cycle starts over.

Almost everything gets overbuilt periodically. Cap rates periodically compress (the rate of return on invested capital gets lower) in an irrational fashion. It is not always possible to buy low and sell high. Trying to find the very top of the market or the very bottom is a fool's errand. However, it is possible to figure out when some segment of the market is genuinely overheated and run the other way (or sell into it if you have the right product). It is also possible to see that an asset is out of fashion and has good cash flow. Even if you plan to own an asset forever, it's possible to wait until it is fairly priced before buying. In summary: buy below replacement cost, not above; build into a rising market, not a falling one. Not very sophisticated, but it works.

Your perspective should be that real estate ownership is not an end in itself, but a vehicle to make money. You should look at every asset you own every year to see if there is a divergence between what you think it's worth and what the market thinks it's worth. If the market price is a lot higher than your price, sell! If assets are selling for less than you calculate they are worth, buy! Certainly there are turnover costs and tax considerations. Certainly, you can also harvest value by driving rents instead of selling. But, in general, every asset you own should always be for sale at some number. One of the best ways to prosper is to allow the irrationality of the marketplace to work on your behalf.

Timing is everything, as I will illustrate with the following story. It's not totally germane, but one of my proudest moments as a public speaker.

I was invited to speak as a so-called outlook breakfast in an upscale suburb or a major West Coast city. There was to be a presenter for each product type—investments, multi-family, industrial, office and retail. I was supposed to come on at the end and say something entertaining and insightful.

Each of the speakers got up and fulfilled the requirement, until we got to the last product speaker—for retail. The guy was named something like Montgomery Montgomery III. Very distinguished looking and very well dressed. It immediately became apparent that he wasn't going to talk about the retail market in general. He was going to tell us about his deal across the street. His family owned a very successful mall. Next door, a large investment shop had started a development and gone upside down in the process with only a large garage finished. Montgomery had bought the deal very cheaply and the garage was a huge plus for his mall. He had just finished the first phase of the new deal with a monster opening for the newest branch of a highly regarded chain. He started out by saying something like, "The three surest paths to success are to be the first born son, the second wife, or the third developer; I managed to hit on two out of three." He then proceeded to tell us about his deal. I got up afterword and started out by saying: "Montgomery, I like your summary of paths to success. But I think I can get you a trifecta. You come back to San Francisco with me and you can be somebody's second wife." At that very moment, the mayor of San Francisco was in the process of creating a political firestorm by legalizing gay marriage in our town without benefit of legislation or judicial decision. Timing is everything. It got a good laugh.

My point in retelling the joke is twofold: to relive my comedic triumph, and to talk about the third developer. A great many projects, especially large and complex deals, only succeed after a write-down and a chance for a market to mature. The first two developers quite often go bust.

5. So You Want to Be a Developer!

Start By Looking at the Risks

I am unaware of any school that can teach you the development business except the proverbial school of hard knocks. Many of the successful developers I know have very little education, and several were thrown out of schools (in the old days when schools did that). I was asked to leave a Jesuit college for being a shit disturber. I managed to talk my way back in and graduate. But I'm a graduate school dropout. The only way I know to learn to do deals is to do some. See how you like the process and if you make any money. If you make money but don't like the process, look for another profession. If you like the process, but don't make money, become an architect.

Development involves four sets of risks (the ability to mitigate risk being the single most important job a developer has). These would be political risk, construction risk, financing risk and marketing risk. In this chapter, we'll talk about construction risk and financing risk. The other two rate chapters of their own.

Construction in this context means the whole process of getting the building up in the air, from assessing the stability of the soil to picking out the type of windows. This is an orchestration process. I once had a boss who used the wrench metaphor. He would call somebody who was good at a particular job a #6 wrench--someone who could skillfully turn a #6 bolt. The developer has (to use another tortured metaphor) to play conductor to an orchestra. You need an architect, a soils engineer, a structural engineer, a fire suppression consultant, a code compliance consultant, an acoustics consultant, etc. I could go on and on. I once built a job on top of a Native American burial ground that was 3,000 years old. I ended up hiring an archeologist, and the chief of the tribe, to help me site the buildings so as not to disturb the burials. You have to get the right players of the right instruments, at the right price, and induce them to play the same tune at the same time. You also have to induce them to play your tune, instead of theirs.

The important thing when picking a consultant is to pick somebody who has a lot of experience doing exactly the thing you want done. Don't pick a podiatrist to perform heart surgery. Get the guy who's worked on a thousand hearts. A good consultant will have professional standards that you need to acknowledge and respect. A good consultant will have productive relationships with your other consultants and with government authorities. Quite often, those relationships may not fully serve your interest, but you have to respect them if you want first class work. The consultant has to do business with the government official long after you're gone. In many cases, your consultant will be doing the bureaucrat's work instead of yours, and you get to pay for it. That is the way the game is played. As with all relationships, showing respect, offering praise, and paying on time will get you a better level of service. Speaking of paying on time, a real problem can develop if you aren't careful. You're getting paid at the end (if and when the deal works); everybody else in the process is getting paid by the hour. Until the construction loan funds, you are reaching into your (undoubtedly shallow) pocket. My preferred method is to get the major consultants to participate in the risk to some extent. They should be willing to do a little preliminary work in good faith to move the process down the road to a feasibility decision. When times are tough, you can often negotiate a two-tier rate. Pay 50% of the standard fee until the deal closes (and no more if it doesn't close) and then, retroactively and forward, pay 125% of the going rate if

Try to avoid hiring an architect with an edifice complex.

the deal goes together. That procedure helps keep everybody's eye on the ball and conscious of costs.

When picking a contractor, you need to look very carefully at track record. How's his/her track record building the kind of building you want to build? There are always lots of surprises in the construction of any building. A contractor who has built a lot of them will have encountered most or the unpleasant surprises in the past, and will therefore be better prepared to deal with them in the future. You also need to check references carefully to see how the contractor responds to adversity. Will he/she bite the bullet and finish the job without trying to change-order you to death? One technique I use is to insist that there be no overhead/profit mark-up on any change-orders. That tends to discourage the practice. You should tell your contractor that he/she had better be satisfied with the working drawings, because you aren't going to sign any change order premised on a misunderstanding of the plans and/or specs. That forces the contractor to confront the architect about any ambiguities in the plans. You should also hire a construction manager, if you're doing a large job, to redline the drawings (mark them up to correct errors and ambiguities; eliminate unnecessarily expensive details) and watch the contractor. If it's a small job and you have a good relationship with the contractor, he/she can redline the plans.

The nightmare of any job is the bankruptcy of the general contractor or any of the subcontractors (subcontractors are plumbers, electricians, drywall hangers, and roofers whom your contractor hires). You need to check out the financial viability of everybody working on the job. You need to see a list of all the subs who are being asked to bid and you should retain the right to veto any of them who you think might go bankrupt.

Finally, you need to find a lawyer who is COMPLETELY current on the state of law and cases regarding lien releases in the jurisdiction in which you're building, and follow his/her instructions to the letter when disbursing construction draws and obtaining releases. At the end of the job, start the lien period promptly and correctly. Nothing will screw up your closing of a sale or permanent financing like a lien. If you get a nuisance lien (blackmail), you can usually bond around it, if you have a proper relationship with your title company and your insurance agent.

Risk is my business and I'm even putting in my own quarter.

How to Go About Raising Equity?

Here's a great line from a friend of mine who peddles multimillion-dollar houses. "Raising money from friends is a hobby; raising money from strangers is a business."

In order to do deals, you are going to need money—equity and debt. In order to induce anybody to lend you money you are going to need a track record. In order to get a track record, you are going to have to do a deal. You can begin to see the circular nature of this process. It is possible that you can get a track record doing deals for somebody else in a development organization, but having your own ass on the line is really the only appropriate apprenticeship. If you really want to learn to be a developer, the best way to do that is to do deals. When you do your first deal, you will need to raise money from people who know you, and can be induced to trust you to return their investment. You will have to raise a major percentage of the cost of the deal, because the lenders won't lend you much, if anything. You may be forced to do your first few deals with sellers who carry back paper (because they can't find another buyer, or another buyer at a price you are willing to pay) or land owners who will stay in the deal for a piece of the upside. In any event, you will have to find equity before you can get debt.

There are brokers who will raise equity for you. It will cost you a lot of money to get the money (meaning you better have a very profitable deal to peddle) and the terms will be very tough (meaning a big slice of the profit, and ugly consequences in the event of failure—including surrender of body parts). You will also have personal liability (all of your assets will be pledged for repayment). Not too big a problem if you have no assets. I have two rules about personal liability. If you have little or nothing, sign lots of guarantees with lots of different lenders and equity partners. If you go down, they can spend their time fighting with each other. If you actually have assets, be very careful to limit the dollar amount of any guarantee you sign to a number for which you are comfortable writing a check. If you have assets, guarantees are really enforceable.

For your first deal or two, you are probably better off doing something small (rehabilitating a little apartment building or buying a beat up house out of probate) and get the necessary money from friends and acquaintances. Keep the amount of each equity contribution fairly small—mostly small in comparison to the net worth of the contributor. Anyone investing with you will be taking a chance; they should not be risking their financial security to take that chance.

The normal deal involves some kind of waterfall. This is true of deals of all sizes, but the waterfall gets very complicated in the big leagues. At the time of a capital event (sale or refinance of the asset you've built or rehabilitated), the first money goes to pay any outstanding bills from third parties. Then, the third party debt gets paid. After that, you might get a developer fee of some kind--4% of hard and soft costs, sometimes excluding land, is fairly common--to reimburse you for overhead. Next the investor gets an agreed return on his/her investment: high single digits is the normal range. After that, the investor gets his/her capital back. Only then do you start to get paid. Profit is then split (maybe 35 to you and 65 to the investor if you're new to the game). Very often, there are IRR triggers. After the investor has received (say) a 12% return, the split gets better for the developer. Maybe there are further triggers at 15 and 20. The important thing to remember, Mr. or Ms. Developer, is that you don't get a cent (except maybe a repayment of your overhead, if you were a tough enough negotiator, and the deal was fat enough on paper, and you have some experience to sell) until everybody else is paid.

Once you've done a few deals (successfully), it gets a lot easier. You have a track record (with real numbers) to sell. At some point, the investors start looking for you. Institutional investors will never admit they are looking for you, but they are.

Dealing with Lenders

When you are borrowing money, it is vitally important to understand the prospective of the principal on the other side of the table. This is true in any negotiation, but especially true when trying to borrow money.

Your prospective lender is not giving you his or her money to use to build or buy your project. You are getting money that was borrowed from somebody else. This is money deposited by checking account customers or savers, from people paying insurance premiums, from 401k or IRA contributions, from public or private pension plans, etc. A few people do lend their own money, but you better hope you never have to borrow from one of them. You'll be paying a very high rate of interest and may get a few bones broken if you miss a payment. Even the hard money lenders who don't break bones are a tough lot.

So... your lender is also a borrower. What is my point? The point is the spread your lender hopes to make between its cost of funds and the amount it is charging you. You have to try to figure out the source and cost of your lender's money and offer terms of repayment that will induce a funding. When times are tough, the lender is most worried about return of funds. You have to demonstrate that you have a good net worth and a good history of repayment. You have to demonstrate that your project has significant equity above the loan amount, so that you can survive a loss of value without going underwater on the loan. You have to demonstrate that you have a secure income stream and/or can dispose of the asset in almost any circumstance for more than the amount of the loan. When times are good, the lender is most worried about return on the funds lent. How much spread and how much fee income can be generated. When times are really good, and there are a lot of lenders competing for your business, the key is volume, because the only way to make significant money is to make a little spread on a lot of loans. Understanding lender motivation (the timing and criteria for the loan officer's bonus) is the key to getting a deal done.

When borrowing money, I almost always use a broker. Lenders have different hot buttons at different times; those hot buttons change all the time; and they are almost never willing to share them. A good broker will know who wants to lend right now; who wants to lend on your kind of project; who has money backed up; and who stands to make a bonus if they get a loan done with you before the end of the fiscal year.

When borrowing money, I do most of the work on flexibility issues. Interest rates are mostly set by the market. Given the quality of the asset, the ratio of loan to value, the strength of the borrower, an interest rate will fall out that will not vary much from lender to lender at any given time. The question then becomes the amount of pre-payment penalty, the rollover options, the ability to substitute collateral, the ability to do a partial pay-down if you sell part of the asset, the level of cross-collateralization (other assets pledged to secure repayment), etc. You want to get all the flexibility you can. Maximize the number of exits you have from the deal. Things can change over the term of the loan, in unexpected ways. It's never the alligator you're watching that bites you in the ass.

If you insist on making "The End of Capitalism As We Know It" a borrower default, I think a 10-day cure period is a little short.

How to Approach a Lender

As I said, I almost always hire a broker when seeking a loan. But you can't leave all the packaging to your broker. You have to participate in the process. Someone from the lender's shop may actually look at the property, but probably not. All they are going to see is your package.

First and foremost, avoid the temptation to write an autobiography. Other than relevant educational experience, relevant work experience and relevant track record, nobody is interested. Your hobbies are immaterial.

Lenders love facts. They are deductive thinkers. That can cause problems for them because they tend to want to lend on projects that are familiar, which means they contribute to overbuilding. Facts are wonderful things, but they are all in the past. Your project will be built, and leased or sold, in the future. Your grasp of macro market trends; your ability to properly position your project; your ability to execute; and pure blind luck will determine your success or failure. A thousand comps (comparable rents and sale prices) won't save you, but that is what the lenders want to see. If there are enough comps, they will be comfortable that your project will succeed.

The package should be thorough and professional. Get all the relevant data and check it twice. The executive summary should be crisp and fully informative, because that may be all the head credit officer will read. But all of it needs to be good, because some junior person reading all the way to the last page could trip you up. Internal consistency is a must. I used to sit on an investment committee full of very smart people. Most of the members spent their time wading through hundred-page packages looking for inconsistencies they could throw in each other's faces. The operative line was "good catch!"

Your loan will go before a committee. I could write a whole book about the dynamics of investment and/or loan committee politics, but we'll save that for another day. I may be old, but I'm still too young to piss off that many people. In general, each committee has its own set of dysfunctions, but there is a common denominator. All the less powerful people on the committee spend their time trying to figure out how the powerful people are going to vote, so they don't end up on the wrong side. If you have a good broker, he/she will know the committee process at the target lender, and know how to work it. If you have a good loan officer, the skids will be greased with the powerful members of the committee before the deal ever gets to a hearing.

If you have preleased your project and it is a quality product in a quality location, you can probably get a loan for 75% of the value when times are good. When times are bad, it will be 75% of cost. When times are really bad, it might be 50% of cost. The rest of the cost will have to be covered with equity (dollars out of your pocket or that of your investors). Equity money has to go in first. You will also have to sign guarantees for a construction loan (the loan on which you make draws to do the construction or acquisition and rehabilitation). There are two kinds of guarantees, one saying you will complete the project even if the loan proceeds aren't sufficient to cover the cost (meaning you have to eat cost overruns, subcontractor bankruptcies, uninsured loss, etc.) and the other a repayment guarantee. I am always willing to sign for completion, because that is, after all, what I am selling—the ability to get it built and the tenacity/integrity to get it built, come hell or high water. Repayment guarantees can often be limited to a set dollar amount, less than the whole value of the loan. If you haven't preleased the project, or it isn't multi-family residential in a strong market, you're only going to be able to do a deal with a lot of equity, a lot of guarantees, and/or a strong balance sheet (meaning that the guarantee is eminently collectable). The only other alternatives are to find a dumb lender or a high interest leg breaker.

One little summary item here: Real estate investment is, in the grand universe of investment, mid-way between a stock and a bond. The bottom 50 to 75% of the capital stack looks like a bond—fixed rate of return and fairly safe. The top of the stack looks like a stock—an estimate of future earnings with a much higher risk and return spectrum.

Two Stories; One lesson

In the 70s and 80s, I was a junior partner with a national development firm. My job was to build industrial buildings in Northern California. Our typical deal involved borrowing about 85% of cost (with a guaranteed leaseback to circumvent California foreclosure laws). In general, we borrowed money in the 9-9.5% range and the free and clear yield on the deals (on a good day) was 10%.

We would then raise about 35% of the cost in the form of equity from limited partners. We offered those partners a 7% cumulative, preferred return (meaning they got all net cash flow from operations, refinance or sale until such time as they had received a 7% IRR), 50% of the profits above that, and (by far the most important) all of the tax benefits. In those days, the top marginal rate was 70%, and investment losses could be used to offset ordinary income. The bulk of the losses came from the depreciation allowance on the buildings and interior improvements. Hardly anybody actually paid 70% of their income in taxes. Anybody who made significant money spent a significant portion of their time and energy looking for loopholes. We were in the loophole business. The investors were happy as long as we delivered the promised losses. If an investor partner got additional profit, it was serendipity.

The result of our deal is that we raised about 120% of cost. If lease-up proceeded according to plan, we bled back about 5%, and kept 15% as real cash profit. After that, the investors got all the cash flow (if there was any) for the first few years. We stood to make additional money on sale or refinance. In an era of high inflation, we stood a good chance for additional returns. It was depreciated money, but the IRR to us was infinite, because we had no cash invested. Of course, when the tax law changed in 1989, the entire development business went in the toilet in a heartbeat. We were all broke; some knew it and some didn't.

However, nobody predicted that the House and Senate would go behind closed doors and lower the top marginal rate from 70 to 28 and build a firewall between investment income (paper losses) and earned income. We had a government induced business plan and we stuck to it. In my case, a lot of the loan money came from a New England-based insurance company that invested its own money (float on policy holder payments) and managed money for pension funds. In 1974, congress passed ERISA (Every Ridiculous Idea Since Adam) which pressed defined benefit pension plans to confront the fact of inflation by diversifying their portfolio. Lots of insurance companies got in the business of managing the money allocated to real estate.

During one of my visits to our primary lender, I was pulled aside by some people who worked the equity side. They wanted to become my partner. While 9.5% might seem like a great return when CDs are paying 1%, it wasn't in 1982, because inflation was running in high single digits. Fixed rate lenders were getting slaughtered. The deal proposed was that I would be provided with 100% of the money required to build a deal, including a 4% developer fee. I was to pay a 10% cumulative return, as available, and 50% of any profit eventually generated. The upside provided their investors with an inflation hedge.

I took this deal back to my bosses. They were aghast—where's the front end pop? My response was that I was getting paid for my time, and trading half the upside for all the downside. Hell, I thought, let's build out the world. If a deal goes great, I get half the profit; if it goes in the toilet, they suffer all the downside.

All of that worked out and I built a lot of deals with a yield of 10% (or better), but the bloodbath was in the details. We ended up having a gaggle of deal points (timing of draws, amount of profit split, reset of cash flow calculations) that we fought over on every deal point. I came to refer to them as the dirty dozen deal points. I won a few of the battles, but lost most of them. I kept hitting the wall of the Golden Rule: He/she who has the gold makes the rules.

About two years after I started doing these deals, another partner in the organization—a high-rise guy—did a deal with the same capital source. There was a big closing dinner to celebrate. Nobody ever suggested a closing dinner to celebrate one of my deals, so I was a bit insulted. However, his one deal had the dollar volume of maybe 10 of mine, and I was aware of the Law of Large Numbers. If you are working for a small percentage (institutional managers of real estate investments typically get a fee of 1% when they do an acquisition, and about 50 basis points annually to manage the investment), the way to make large money is to do large deals. So, I was invited to fill out a large table in the private dining room of an historic San Francisco restaurant to celebrate the closing of a large deal.

During the course of dinner, I learned that my high-rise brother had completely prevailed in his negotiation of each and every one of the dirty dozen deal points. Several other institutional investors had been courting him to do the deal. Every time there was any pushback, he mentioned that fact. My equity partners, for whom I had produced a number of very profitable deals, gave away the store to partner with a guy who had produced nothing for them--because there was competitive pressure. By the bye, his deal eventually went completely in the toilet.

Now, a second tale with the same cast of players. I had a deal with them in which we invested in a large tract of land on the periphery of the market. We got enough land to build a 2.5 million foot industrial park with a significant carry-back from the seller at $18,000 per acre. The hooks were that it was going to take some time and a lot of work on the soils to bring the deal to fruition. At some point, my boss was feeling poorly and wanted the cash we had invested back out of the deal. He told me to visit the home office of our partner and trade some of our interest in the project for the cash. After a day of truly brutal negotiation, I called him. My message was that I could get the deal done but that every part of our corporate body would be scorched in the process. Cash, at all cost, was the response. So, I went, with hanging head, into the office of my negotiating adversary and told him that, my advice notwithstanding, we would take his deal. I also complimented him on kicking every square inch of my ass. His response: "That's what you get for only having one source."

As a result of those two experiences, my iron rule is that, when it comes to both debt and equity, it pays to have more than one source of funds. Nothing motivates a lender like competition. The motivation is especially strong when the allocation has not been fully placed and the fiscal year is coming to an end.

Two More Stories; One More Lesson

During one period of my career, I worked for a company that invested funds in real estate on behalf of public and private pension plans, university endowments and wealthy individuals. Our specialty was industrial buildings and neighborhood retail, because the average deal size was about $10 million. We were in that niche because the Law of large Numbers left those two property types available. The big dogs did not want to bother. My job, among other things, was to be the Exalted Vice President In Charge of All the Screwed Up Deals in the System. We had taken over a lot of business from other advisors, which they had screwed up, and we bought a lot of wounded deals that we thought could be healed. I was the medic.

The comfort of having several money sources available.

In one case, we were buying a large portfolio from two bottom feeders in Texas. At the nadir of the real estate debacle that comprised the early 90s, they had convinced some investors to back them in assembling a bunch of industrial deals in Texas and Oklahoma. They had bought at maybe 30% of replacement cost; we were under contract to buy most of the Texas stuff and maybe 50% of replacement cost (at a time when the market was beginning to recover). The key point in the story has me driving around Houston, with my brick-sized cell phone, looking at the buildings in question. I arrived at one little gaggle of grade level (no dock high loading) buildings in an unfortunate part of town, which precipitated a call to the boss. I said you've got to throw this crap out of the package, or words to that effect. He asked me why. I summarized by saying that the anchor tenant was in the business of relining brakes on forklifts, which created a cloud of asbestos; that finding replacement tenants for the deadbeats in occupancy, when they inevitably went broke, might take the rest of the century; and that the current owners had neglected to repaint after the last flood, leaving a high water mark about 14 feet up the walls. He promptly dismissed my concerns by saying that I was getting paid to solve problems like that; and that the sellers had no investor partners in that project, meaning that their level of horniness to close the deal (and tolerance for a haircut at the last minute) would be significantly diminished if they weren't salivating over the projected return from that deal. The light bulb above my head duly went on. I did eventually win the argument by saying that nothing I could do would prevent our competitors from driving a pension fund investor by the building, and successfully badmouthing us, but his point was taken in any event.

The second story involves the Initial Public Offering of that very same company. A very complicated undertaking which involved a large number of institutional investors (80-some, if recollection serves) trading their ownership in properties under our management for shares to be issued by our new company. IPOs are inherently difficult processes and ours was worse than most in terms of moving parts. About March or April of the year we went public, the boss announced that the roll out date would be in late November. That announcement created an uproar. The consensus was that we couldn't possibly get everything done in that time frame. I went to the boss's office and closed the door. I asked him why he set the deadline. He said, "Bonuses are paid on Wall Street at the end of November." I nodded and went back to work.

The moral of the story is that people do what they get paid to do. If you can figure out how a lender or equity provider gets paid, and craft your proposal to maximize the prospect of a payday, you will get more money and get it faster and get it with fewer strings attached.

A Word About Build-to-Suits

Almost all developers lust after build-to-suits. That's an arrangement whereby a user of office or retail or industrial space contracts to buy, or lease (on a long term basis) a building to be built to its specifications. It seems like an ideal way for a developer to make money. The marketing risk is eliminated; you know in advance who is going to occupy the building. Most of the financing risk is eliminated. In a presale, all you need is a construction loan for a few months. With a leased investment, you can usually get a commitment for a takeout to fund at CO (award of Certificate of Occupancy from the relevant authority) at a rate set in advance if you pay a few points for the commitment. Most of the political risk is eliminated. Politicians and planning bureaucrats love users. They especially love big, creditworthy users (build-to-suits don't usually get done with any other kind), because they promise to bring jobs and tax revenue. The difference in attractiveness (politician-wise) between a spec building (built for tenants to be obtained later), which will eventually be occupied by users who generate jobs and tax revenue, and a building that is preleased, has always baffled me. Nevertheless, I have almost never encountered a significant problem getting planning approval for a build-to-suit, except in left-leaning jurisdictions that want no construction of any kind.

So the only risk you think you have if you can get a user signed up is construction risk. What could be better?

Actually, there are two significant risks associated with build-to-suits. The first is what I will call margin risk. If you are proposing to build a speculative building, you will need a track record and equity. Anyone lending you money or investing with you will want some assurances that you know what you're doing and that the deal has a significant margin. The build-to-suit developer needs none of that. If you have the presale document or the lease document duly signed and in hand, you are bankable. Meaning that there is no barrier to entry. Cheapest bid wins. In numerous cases I've observed, developers will bring land they own into a build-to-suit quote at what they paid for it years before. Meaning that they completely ignored their cost of capital.

I remember sitting in a very unpleasant investment committee meeting about a proposed deal with a major user for an industrial building to be constructed adjacent to a major airport. The guy who made the quote did the math on an international flight, when he was sleep deprived, and he made a serious mathematical error. We determined that we would lose significant money if we stood by the quote. The finished building, leased at the rent proposed, would be worth significantly less than our cost to produce the building. The cause of the agony was threefold:

1. We were anxious to develop a relationship with the tenant in question.

2. We were anxious to deepen a relationship with the airport authority.

3. We were embarrassed.

After lots of emotion-laden dialogue, we voted to stand by the quote. We lost the deal to somebody who came in lower.

Build-to-suits tend to get bid aggressively, and the winning bidder is almost always somebody who is working very, very thin (or several feet underwater).

When I was building a lot of industrial property in Northern California in the 80s, a guy walked in my door unannounced and asked if I could build a vault for travelers' checks and associated offices on land our company owned in Foster City, CA. For you younger folk, travelers' checks were what we carried on trips before there were ATMs. When cosigned by the holder, they were the equivalent of cash. If they were lost or stolen, the issuer would theoretically replace them promptly. I explained to my guest that I could not accommodate him in Foster City because the whole town was built on fill atop San Francisco Bay. A building as heavy as a 20,000-square-foot vault would sink right into the mud if not built (at great cost) on deep piles. I told him that I had some land in a community a few miles north that would accommodate a heavy building. We got right into my truck to look at the dirt. He told me that he had to get twenty facilities, worldwide, built in the next few months. Eventually, he even told me how much rent he was willing to pay. We did a deal; we used the facility to anchor a small, upscale industrial park; we sold out to a syndicator shortly after lease up; we made a lot of money. I had the right piece of land in the right place to accommodate a man in a hurry; and I could make good money at his budgeted number, which he was happy to give me because his salient hot button was speed of delivery.

No decent build-to-suit deal was ever done unless the developer had a hook. Here are a few examples of good "hooks:" You have a tenant who has several years to go on a lease that you can tear up. You have the piece of land that works better than any land your competitors can bring to the table. You are the only one who has the expertise and fortitude to get the political approvals. You are the only one who can produce the building in the time frame required. You have pictures of the CEO engaged in sex with a shapely ewe. My advice to those who don't have a hook is to throw the Request for Proposal in the wastebasket. If you don't, you may very well get the business and go broke if one little thing goes sideways.

The second major risk is what I call estoppel risk. An estoppel is a statement from a tenant for benefit of a lender saying that a lease is in full force and there is no landlord default. Prior to completing your sale to the user or an investor, or prior to your closing your takeout loan, the provider of money will demand an estoppel from your user. Your user will understand that, without a clean estoppel, you are in developer hell. At which point, the wish list comes out. Everything the user forgot to put in the specs, or thought up during construction; every minor dispute you thought you'd settled; and every rationalization for extraction imaginable will come out of the woodwork. Since you, Mr. Developer, have virtually no leverage in this situation, you will be serving up every item on the wish least free of charge and with a smile on your face. The moral of this story is to be damn careful when the estoppel clause is being negotiated. Build in some penalties for failure of timely performance. Also build in some slack in your sale or takeout documentation so that a less than perfect estoppel will be sufficient for funding.

Some Thoughts About Value Creation

Unless you are buying an asset encumbered by a long-term net lease (in which case, you are basically buying a bond), any transaction you do should be designed to create value. If you are building something, the value of the finished product should exceed the cost of land, construction, interest and consultants. If you are buying something, you should be bringing some expertise to the table that will render the asset more valuable in real dollars over the holding period.

Value creation is one of the two basic tenants of capitalism. If you don't create value, there is no profit. The Union of Soviet Socialist Republics was the great controlled experiment in economic planning. In theory, the economy was owned by the people, and run for their benefit. The central planners allocated raw materials, established production quotas, and set the price of finished goods. The eventual result was a destruction of value. They took valuable leather and turned it into worthless shoes. In my opinion, we didn't win the Cold War. The inexorable logic of the system caused the enemy to implode. In my opinion, any participant in the economy who does not create value is responsible for impoverishing the society. Any employee must generate more value than the salary and benefits being paid to him or her in order to continue in the employ of a sane employer. The reason to oppose socialism and state capitalism and collusive capitalism is that those systems destroy value and eventually destroy the economy.

The other, and infinitely more important, tenet of capitalism is bankruptcy. It is the true genius of our system. If you fail to create value, you get to go broke and start over. Failure is punished. The common mistake made in the critique of capitalism is that it is all about profit. Wrong! Lots of socialist enterprises make money, especially since lots of them are insulated from competition. But the ones that fail to make money are kept in business anyway. There is no penalty for failure. Leading some famous person to say (approximately) that the problem with socialism is that you eventually run out of other people's money.

Every real estate transaction you do needs to be viewed from the prism of the value that you create during your tenure of ownership.

In some cases, success is as simple as getting in the way of the big wave. If you bought land in or around Los Angeles in 1950, you made money. Millions of people migrated to Southern California between 1950 and 1990. All you had to do was get in the way of the hoard to make out. I blame it all on the Rose Bowl. Almost every January 1, it was 70 degrees, and the San Gabriel Mountains were clearly visible in the panoramic shots. At 5:00 PM EST, some poor fool in Buffalo, who had spent the day shoveling snow, turned on the TV to see fans in shirt sleeves and cheerleaders wearing very little. His response was to tie the mattress to the roof of the car and move south and west. At one point in the 1950s, there was an annual picnic at a park in Long Beach that drew thousands of migrants from Iowa. Just Iowa.

If you buy raw land and get it entitled for single-family lots, you have usually created value. The total price you will receive for selling the lots will significantly exceed the cost of the land, the cost of consultants, the cost of carry, and the cost of your time.

If you buy land, do the entitlements, put up a building and rent it, you should have an income stream that will sell for more than the money you spent to create the asset.

If you find a beat up asset in a decent neighborhood, and rehabilitate it to the point where it will attract tenants who create an institutional-grade income stream, you can create a lot of value. You should have started out with a double-digit cap rate appropriate to non-institutional grade property, and ended up with a cap rate appropriate to institutional grade property. If you are applying a lower cap rate to a larger income stream, there is a lot of pop.

There is value in timing and fads, commonly known as grave dancing. Bubbles collapse; product types and locations go out of fashion; liquidity disappears. As one of my former bosses said, big money in real estate is made by those who have cash to invest when nobody else does. If you have money or can raise money, and can buy when everybody else is desperate to sell, there is value to be created. The important metric is replacement cost-- replacement cost properly calculated. That means the price you pay for an asset plus the money necessary to render the asset functionally and aesthetically equivalent to new construction. You may not be physically able to convert the asset to like-new condition, in which case the income stream projection needs to reflect a spread to new asset rents. If you can buy an asset at well below replacement cost (properly calculated), and you are in a location that will not deteriorate during your ownership tenure, value is created.

Value can be created by arbitrage. On a regular basis, the public markets and the private markets attribute different values to similar streams of income. If the public market is paying more, form a REIT. If the private market is paying more, do a leveraged buyout of a public vehicle. Obviously, the spread has to be sufficient to pay the transaction costs and cover the timing risk, but a lot of money has been made by those working that particular arbitrage. You don't even have to be a big player to play this game. Periodically, the implied cap rate of assets in the NAV (net asset value) calculation applied to REIT stock gets to a number that makes little sense. That's the time to buy REIT stock. The time to get out is when that cap rate gets significantly lower than assets of the type the

REIT in question holds are selling for in the private markets.

The final driver I'll mention is the movement of money. When I was in the Navy, I was sent to Virginia Beach to attend a school to learn how to direct naval gunfire. Outside of class time, I spent a lot of time misbehaving. I figured that there was not much threat of sanctions for my behavior, since I already had orders to report to the 1st Marine Regiment in DaNang. On weekends, I went to Maryland or DC, because no alcohol was sold in Virginia on Sundays. When in DC, I gravitated to Georgetown, the site of whatever action there was to be had. Even while inebriated, I could tell that big things were happening in Georgetown from a real estate prospective. The term applied was gentrification. Houses were being repaired and sold to people who were significantly more affluent than prior owners. The demographic was going upscale. When I got out of the service and returned to San Francisco, I encountered the early beginnings of the same phenomenon. In the 1950s and 60s, middle class people had fled the City for the suburbs in San Mateo, Marin and Alameda Counties. Stately Victorian buildings in San Francisco were now occupied by recent immigrants and the underclass. In many cases, Victorian trim work was stripped from the buildings and the exteriors were clad with stucco or (heaven forbid) flagstone. I actually bought one building with 10-foot ceilings, in which dropped acoustic ceilings had been installed. After a brief stint as a commodity broker, I decided that I would return to my roots in the real estate trade. My partners and I bought two- and three-unit buildings in middlin' neighborhoods; upgraded wiring, plumbing, kitchens and baths; and slapped on a lot of white paint. The tenants who responded to our ads were young professionals, seeking out urban amenities and excitement. Value was created because more money was chasing the same square footage.

6. A Short Course in Negotiations

Buy the Book

This is a very important chapter, but I'm not going to devote many words to communicating my insights to you. The reason being that I got most of my good ideas on this subject out of one book. *You Can Negotiate Anything* by Herb Cohen. I had the privilege of hearing Herb speak on several occasions. Cohen is a very funny guy. He covers lots of important bases in his Magnum Opus:

1. The power of standard forms

2. The power of setting deadlines

3. The power of ignoring the other side's deadlines

4. The usefulness of setting a bracket

5. The reason you fail when negotiating with your kids

I haven't read his book in 30 years, but I still remember a lot of it. Aside from being vitally interested in what he had to say, the reason it's fresh in my mind is that I read the book at least three times, and heard him talk about it on several occasions. The keys to retention (even for the elderly) are concentration and repetition. All the talk you hear about multi-tasking is pure bullshit. If you want to learn something, focus completely and repeat. I can still remember how to field strip an M-15 rifle because I learned to do so (repeatedly) before going into a combat zone carrying one such rifle.

The key line in the whole book is: "Ya gotta care... but not that much." My way of saying that is, "He or she who cares least... wins." The only way to successfully negotiate is to drain the proceeding of emotional content (which is why you never win when negotiating with your kids).

"No" is such a weak opening position.

Another Way to Say the Same Thing

One mental construct I use to approach the negotiating process is to focus on the two salient questions in any business negotiation (and in a lot of personal/social negotiation as well):

1. Who is the hostage?

2. How much is the ransom?

It may be that I have become overly cynical (heaven forbid) in my old age, or the subconscious influence of paternal grandmother (a mail-order-bride from Sicily), but

I find that this mental construct has powerful explanatory value in most situations.

If the other team has the hostage and the price is reasonable, pay the price and go on about your business. No agonizing required. If the hostage is overpriced, tell the holder to go ahead and kill it. By the way, never take a hostage you're unwilling to kill. If the other team senses that you're unwilling to kill the hostage if you don't get the ransom, you're not negotiating; you're begging.

Most transactions are a little more complex. Both sides have one or more hostages. The key is to price all of them properly and determine how much "boot" will be paid to the side with the more valuable hostage or hostages.

My view of this process leads me to a bifurcated negotiating style. If I know the adversary and find him/her trustworthy, based on prior experience or solid references, we do a "handshake" deal. There may be paperwork, but it is simple and straightforward. I am assuming that my negotiating partner will perform as promised. If I don't trust the adversary, harsh penalties (and, hopefully, major gotchas inserted by my clever attorney that remain masked until it's too late) are included in the papering of the transaction. Think of it as a drug deal. Both sides arrive heavily armed. The side with the drugs brings a counterfeit expert to examine the cash; the side with the money brings a chemist to test the purity of the drugs. When both sides are satisfied that the ransom terms have been met, there is a simultaneous exchange. Then, both sides retreat, walking backwards.

A Third Way to Say the Same Thing

Lots of people offering advice about negotiating talk about "win-win" outcomes. Horseshit! Negotiating is not about winning; it's about getting what you need. If both sides need the same thing at the same price, nothing works. You have land. I have a plan to put something on the land that will render it more valuable than my projected costs -- if I can buy the land at the right price. If your non-negotiable price (ransom) is at or below my price, we have a deal. If not, I have to tell you to go ahead and kill the hostage (try selling the land to someone who is willing to overpay). If you really need the money (my hostage) to pay your lender; or produce a return for your investors; or just to buy groceries, your price will probably come down to meet my offer.

The key element on which to fix your attention is *needs*. I have one or more core needs when arriving at the negotiating table. I can't buy the land unless it's priced in such a fashion that I think I can make a profit if I buy it. Maybe I can be bamboozled into paying more, but I'll soon be in another business. You have a need (or desire) to turn the value of your land into negotiable currency. The successful negotiation means that both needs are met. It may be that you need a price for your land that gives you bragging rights at the country club or in the press that I can't meet. You may need a symbolic number to feed to your long-suffering investors. In that case, I ask you to carry a significant piece of the price in the form of a loan for a few years at a very low rate of interest, or I offer you a low number for now, but a profits participation in my development deal that could be projected to get your price eventually. We both cast around to see if we can find a place where each of our needs is met. The clever negotiator relentlessly studies the adversary to find out what his/her needs really are (as opposed to the needs he/she puts on the table). Thorough preparation and careful listening will often get you what initially appears impossible to obtain. Success is not "win-win." Success is getting what you really need out of the negotiation and ignoring the rest.

Sitting Bow lets the deal come to him.

The Art of Bluffing

Lots of big dogs (mostly males) fancy that they can win through intimidating their negotiating partners. Mostly, they are deluded. Experienced players can intimidate amateurs, but most significant deals involve experienced people on both sides of the table. My method of dealing with blowhards is try to induce them to run headlong into a pit by pretending that they have me on the run.

In the early 1990s, the commercial real estate market was well and truly in the toilet. The 1986 tax legislation had killed us, but we kept building because the dying S&Ls and the Japanese kept pouring money into the market. From 1985 to 1990, we built 10 years' worth of product. Being a developer in 1991 was the equivalent of being a journeyman buggy whip maker. I did some workout business and supplemented the covering of my run rate by working as an expert witness. Real estate recessions are boom times for litigation. Everybody sues everybody. Most people dread being deposed. I love it! Especially if I am getting paid by the hour (lawyers are the greatest wasters of time imaginable and there are innumerable opportunities for double dipping if you carry a phone and laptop) and there is no liability. Conflict for its own sake! Gun-fighting with blanks!

Some years later, when I had formed our little development company, my partner got asked to do an expert witness gig and asked me for advice. He was representing a small time developer who had undergone a botched operation, which had robbed him of almost all of his sight. He claimed that he could not earn a living without his eyesight. The hospital's lawyers contended that he could hire appraisers to be his eyes. My response was that was fatuous in the extreme. The job of a developer is to make a good estimate of tomorrow's value; the best an appraiser can do is tell you yesterday's value. My partner, a master negotiator, had a more subtle response. He said that he would be unable to stay in business if he was blinded because he would be unable to negotiate with anyone he couldn't see.

Bluffing is for poker. And the reason it works is that the bettor doing the bluffing does not have to show his/her cards if the bluff is not called. Other players have to pay to look. In the non-casino world, the cards always get turned up. If you bluff, you will get caught, and nobody will want to do business with you ever again.

A quick aside on sunk cost. If you are in a negotiation that you really want to conclude successfully, and you are far apart, the way to increase your chances is to run the clock. String things out. Find some things you can agree on. Induce the other team to invest time and, more importantly, money in the process. The heavier the investment, the greater the chances that there will be enough bending at the end to get the deal done. Investment of time and energy are like investments of money in the sense that most people hate to get off a loser. There is a mountain of research demonstrating that almost all investors (professional traders excepted) tend to hang on to losing stock and bond positions hoping for a comeback. We sell winners and keep losers. On the flip side, you should be willing to walk from a negotiation at any stage. Don't let the investment of time or energy or money induce you to chase bad money with good.

So, You Think You're Smart

During part of my Navy career, I served on an elderly rust bucket of a Destroyer Escort wallowing around in the northern reaches of the Pacific watching for the launch of Russian ICBMs. My division consisted of deck apes and gunners' mates. Not the brightest pennies in the collection. You had to flunk the IQ test or be just out of the brig to end up in my charge.

On a ship with long deployments (which we had), there is a lust for shore liberty (which involved a lot of lust). The center of attention toward the end of a long voyage is who would get off the ship when it tied up. We were organized into three sections. One third of the troops had to stay aboard the first day in port to man the ship in the event of an emergency. Those poor souls could get ashore on day one if they convinced another sailor to sign a piece of paper (called a chit) agreeing to act as a replacement. Actually, it took three chits. Somebody had to act as a warm body; somebody had to be qualified to man your station if the ship had to get underway; and somebody had to stand your watches. One person could perform more than one function, but all three had to be covered. We were coming into a desirable port after a long haul (Bangkok, if recollection serves) and there was a frenzy to pull liberty. I got a veritable blizzard of chits to approve. I taped all of them up on the bulkhead of the junior officers' quarters and started drawing some lines. I eventually figured out that every man in the division had submitted multiple chits, the net effect of which was that, if approved, would leave exactly zero sailors on board. A majestic mathematical exercise pulled off by a group of people none of whom were theoretically as smart as yours truly. Had it not been for the existence of similar pranks in past, and my generally suspicious nature, they'd have gotten away with it.

The moral of the story is that attention span beats IQ almost every time. When I worked for a sophisticated investment management operation, we did a lot of joint ventures with developers. My smart colleagues always thought they could paper the transactions in such a fashion that they would secure a disproportionate share of the gain (or pass off a disproportionate share of the risk) from our partners. As a developer who had been on the other side of the table, I had to assure them that the fool in the field would righteously read the paperwork looking for wiggle room, and would cut every corner possible to even up (and then some) long after the clever contract was sitting unread in our file drawers. A much better and safer strategy would be to properly align incentives, and allow the developers to make whatever they could, as long as we were sharing in the upside. Unfair treatment begets unfair treatment. Straight shooting tends to get better results. If, in any given instance, that is not the case, the solution is to get a different partner.

At a strategic moment, the unvarnished truth is a disarming negotiating tactic.

The Proper Negotiating Attitude

Last, but by no means least, you should NEVER appear to have "won" a negotiation. Always trade dignity for dollars. When you've shaken hands and the ink on the paper is dry, spend a lot of time telling the folks on the other side of the table (and their lawyers) how smart they are. Tell them they kicked your ass. Slink out of the room with shoulders barely above the floor. Never brag about winning. All you will accomplish is to create the desire to even up.

7. The Fine Art of Selling

The instinctive response of a great many readers of this minor tome to the word "salesman" will be negative. If you are old enough, the mental image will be of a bullhorn voiced fellow touting the virtues of a used car, with a dog resting on its hood, during the Late, Late Movie. If you are a sophisticated type, the image that will jump into your mind will be "Death of a Salesman" or "Glengarry, Glenross." You assume that the process of selling involves a barrage of pushiness and false claims. Someone saying whatever it takes to get the ink on the dotted line. You would be wrong. No product moves unless it is sold. Even religion is sold. They call it missionary work. Selling is the grease that allows the wheels and gears of the economy to turn. Almost all buying decisions involve change. Change is always frightening. Selling is the process of overcoming that fear. As I said earlier, most people end up doing what they feel like doing. Most analysis is ex post facto rationalization. You've decided what you want to do. You then commission a study that confirms the efficacy of your decision.

What sales people bring to the table is fluency in emotional communication. They call it spotting the buying signals. Detecting the presence of feelings of fear and greed. In my own estimation, I am worthless at selling. I can make the pitch, but I have no real idea how it is being received. If I run a tag team (televised wrestling matches in the 50s used to feature matches between pairs of contestants called tag teams because they had to tag in order to replace combatants in the ring) presentation with a salesperson beside me, I will get a report at the end to let me know which part of the presentation sold and which didn't. I will be told the shape of the prospective buyer's hot buttons; how to find them; how often to push.

It's fairly easy to underwrite selling skills. The large real estate brokerage houses administer personality tests to spot future salespeople. The appropriate psychological markers are high ambition and high socialization. The managers of the big shops tell me that the tests are very predictive. Sales people are born, not made. Either you speak emotion or you don't. The most obvious outward sign is persistence. The sale usually gets made on the fourth, fifth, sixth or seventh call. Those unwilling to make that many calls don't make it. A second sign is the ability to deal with rejection and keep going. Ninety percent (or more) of a salesperson's life consists of being told "no way!" If you can't hack that, you starve. The easiest was to confirm sales ability is really simple. It's money. Good salespeople make lots of money. The best broker I ever met had a very simple rule. He calculated the cost of a desk (the amount of money required to support one sales person in terms of rent, insurance, phone bill, etc.) and multiplied by two (since he was taking ½ the commission up to a fairly large dollar amount). That amount was the cutoff point for working in his shop. If you didn't bill that much, you were gone. Veterans got an occasional one-year pass in a bad market, but two years below the threshold and you were gone, no questions asked or answered, no exceptions made. Good brokers lined up to work for him, because the splits above the base amount were generous, and the support was ample.

The key to turning selling potential into commission dollars is the ability to close. I used to do a little sales training for a medium-sized Silicon Valley broker in the 70s. He had the 1,000-foot rule. That was 1,000 square feet of industrial space. The office equivalent would be about 250 square feet. His view was that the first month in the business a new broker was qualified to do a 1,000-foot deal. After a year, maybe he could do a 10,000-foot deal. After 3 years, 40,000. The idea was to get in the habit of closing. A very good idea. Sometimes, the worst thing that can happen to a young broker is to close a big deal early on, before the closing habit is firmly ingrained.

From a real estate salesperson's point of view, closing has occurred when all parties have signed all the documents; the buyer or lesser has taken possession of the premises; consideration has been exchanged; the commission has been paid; and the money has been buried in the salesperson's backyard.

Another way of saying the same thing is my rule of lists. A broker (or developer or investor, for that matter) should make a list of the deals he/she is working on. Write down the odds of closing each of the deals. Most people with a few years in the business have a pretty good idea of the chances of closing. The more you work on it, the better you get. Once all the deals are rated, rearrange the list with the 90/10s on top and the 10/90s on the bottom. Fold the paper in half; tear it; and throw away the bottom half. In other words, work only on deals that work. Even if the big dollar deals are on the bottom, a 10% chance of big bucks is a good chance to waste time. Even if somebody else eventually makes that deal, you will be ahead because you will have closed a lot of other deals in the interim.

Marketing

Before we spend more time on selling, we need to back up. Before selling comes marketing. Marketing is the process of figuring out where your product fits into the universe of wants. Who might buy your product and why? What price will be a sufficient inducement to generate willing buyers? With respect to real estate, a lot of the questions are answered by location and configuration of the product. Warehouse users want to be close to transportation nodes. Retailers want to be in the flow of shopping traffic. Office users usually want to be close to their home and next to their most prestigious competitors. In suburban office, criterion #1 usually rules. In downtown, it's criterion #2. When you contemplate buying or building a project, a lot of market research and market thinking should precede any financial commitment. It's fairly easy to figure out where to buy or build a high-rise. CBDs (central business districts) are fairly easy to find. Then, the question becomes the history of absorption and rents. Assuming that there is sufficient demand to fill your building, you have to figure out if the market rent will be sufficient to justify the cost of the proposed building. Then, you have to figure out what the building should look like. What sort of finish and floor plate configuration will be attractive to the largest possible proportion of prospective tenants?

Marketing also means looking beyond the first lease. It has been my experience that flexible design is the greatest protection you can get. It is a whole lot easier to get into a deal than get out of one. The exit process is facilitated if you have many ways out. If you can lease or sell; if you can rent all or part; if you have set it up as a condo; if it works for a variety or users; you have a better chance of getting out alive. Specialized real estate and locations off the beaten path will kill you.

About 15 years ago, I did my first deal in Mexico. We connected with a local partner who had a build-to-suit in tow for a Fortune 50 client. It was 750,000 square feet, a double-digit free-and-clear yield! A piece of land under contract! All they needed was our money. The only problem with the deal was that the proposed building was an abortion. It followed the shape of the land parcel, which was a distorted trapezoid. I told our prospective partner that I would not do the deal unless we bought some more land and designed a rectangular building that loaded from both sides. They responded that the user did not care about double loading and buying more land would lower the return on the deal. I responded that I did not want to own a building that would be an albatross around my neck after the seven-year lease term expired. Finding a single user for 750,000 feet of odd shaped concrete would severely limit our universe of prospects. If we built the building I had in mind, it could be cut into 100,000-foot increments, allowing us to talk to a lot more prospects. As it turned out, the user decided they needed another 100,000 feet while we were under construction. We were able to lengthen the building to meet their needs, while preserving divisibility. As it further turned out, the user bought the building, but the value of proper configuration will survive for the entire life of the structure, which is liable to exceed 50 years.

The selling effort should always be preceded by a marketing effort. At every stage of the process, you and your salesperson should have a serious marketing discussion that analyzes all available facts about absorption history, rent level history, and cap rate history. Figure out if you are in the path of progress or in its dust. Is the neighborhood getting better or worse? Do you need to alter the product to get a configuration which sells? Who are your target users/buyers? Given the number of consultants in the business and the plethora of information available on the web, there is plenty of raw material from which to make sound decisions. A good salesperson will help you look for the most relevant data and the appropriate conclusions to draw from the data.

The one thing you can't rely on a salesperson for is the final judgment on rent levels or sales price. Since he/she has a vested interest in telling you what you want to hear in that area, do your own research, and come to your own conclusions. The standard shuck for an agent seeking a listing is to propose an asking price that meets or exceeds your expectations. The agent with the highest proposed asking price gets the listing, and he/she usually pushes for the longest time frame possible on the listing. The listing sits there for a while and becomes stale. Then, your lying agent explains that the only way to induce a fresh look from prospective buyers is a substantial price reduction. Magically enough, the property promptly moves. If you had picked an honest agent and a realistic price to begin with, the result would have been a quicker sale at a higher price. You let the greed bug bite you. Shame on you!

Underwriting Salespeople

At one point in my working life, I traveled around the country for an investment advisor picking out listing agents and property managers for the projects we owned. With respect to industrial property in major urban centers, it was my experience that the average submarket was about 40,000,000 square feet. That market would have some kind of geographic and marketing coherence. It would relate to some transportation node (port, airport, freeway junction, etc.) and have a fairly coherent set of users. My arrival in town would always elicit a flood of calls from brokers looking for a listing. Brokers have a good grapevine. I once worked a property in Manhattan and it was like dealing with jungle drums from a 50s movie about Africa. The brokers knew I was coming as a walked the streets from office to office. It was eerie. When conducting that kind of exercise, the question I asked each broker was, "if not you, who should I list with?" Asking that question enough times will yield a short list. In any given submarket, there are four or five people doing most of the business. In selling, the 80/20 (or maybe even 90/10) rule really does apply. A few people do almost all the business. Once I figure out who the few people are, it becomes a matter of picking one of them. In markets where I had a large presence, I gave a listing to all of them. In markets where I had small presence, I tried to pick the one that was most trusted by the others.

In general, you will get most of your leases and buyers from a very identifiable group of prospects who will be represented by the brokers who do most of the business in the submarket in which you have product. Your job is to pick a broker who is in the small group of real producers and insist that he/she be in regular contact with the other producers. You might occasionally get a user from outside the herd represented by a broker from outside the herd, but you will waste your time designing a marketing plan with that eventuality in mind. This is why I said earlier, Work on deals that work; don't work on deals that aren't liable to work.

The Care and Feeding of Salespeople

Your aim here is twofold: immediate gratification and recognition. When I was leasing a lot of space, my pledge to the brokers was that they would have a check in their hands within 24 hours of my receipt of a signed lease and deposit. When I worked a specific geographic area in the 1970s and 80s, I hand-delivered the checks—walked them thru the cubes attached to a Mylar balloon. Nothing frustrates a salesperson more than getting a deal across the finish line and then waiting for weeks or months for their commission. If you are the quickest pay, you will get the most showings, and the inside information necessary to get the most deals done.

Recognition is almost as important as money. In any selling organization, there is a recognition scheme. Watch the movie "Tin Men." Proceeds from the first sale go to buy a Caddy, because that is the way one salesman proves to another that he is a success. Sales organizations have territories, quotas, extra rewards for good producers, cruise junkets for top producers. Salespeople have high socialization. They want to have defined goals and be recognized for meeting or exceeding those goals. After you've paid the commission, buy an ad in the local business rag to thank the salesperson. Put their name in big letters; yours in small letters. Get a picture of the building with a nice frame and a little plaque thanking your salesperson for the transaction that he/she can display on the desk. Many years ago, I bought a building from a Fortune 100 company, which involved a short-term carry-back for part of the purchase price. The seller shorted the broker's commission pending payment of our debt. I bought him a very early version of a cell phone (actually a Motorola radio) to express my appreciation for his work and apologize for the stiffing he took. Long after I had forgotten the whole thing, I called him to ask for a favor. He responded that for some period of time, he was the only broker in his market with a mobile phone, and that he still thought fondly of me. Needless to say, he responded generously to my request. A small gesture reaped big dividends. Salespeople spend their lives dealing with people who do not respect them or their calling; you can make a lot of hay offering a little respect.

Occasional Surgery

There are lots of deals that won't work without some haircuts being administered. It is often necessary to negotiate the commission downward in order to get the numbers to work. I refer to it as "fee-ectomy." It is a delicate operation. Most market participants start the cutting way too soon. If you have a need to perform the operation (whether it be renegotiating a purchase price or adjusting the amount of a commission), wait until the last minute, when the stench of a closing is in the nostrils of all the participants. The pitch should be, "I'm willing to go forward, and put my cash on the table, but we will all have to make a contribution in order to get the numbers to work." If you cut skillfully and apologize, the person on the operating table will still be talking to you at the end of the day. And will probably come back to do more business with you. Most of the money is better than none. On large transactions, all the fees are negotiable, and the participants all grow their hair in preparation. On several occasions, when the numbers were close but not there, I have offered to share the pain three ways—buyer, seller and broker. That approach has worked, if I have been able to demonstrate that I have a rational basis for asking for the haircut.

Selling to Institutional Money

Much of the capital for commercial real estate is provided by institutional investors—pension funds and their advisors (including funds run by the big investment banks), university endowments, private equity funds, etc. Selling to these entities is a field unto itself.

In order to raise money from institutional investors, a carefully calibrated marketing/selling program is required. The salesperson has to be "one of the crowd." The target audience is usually no more than a few score players. Your salesperson must be familiar to them. That's the only way to get the door opened or the call answered. Your offering must be targeted to the allocation the investor is trying to fill. Most funds are allocated based on an RFP (Request for Proposal) process, which is tightly defined. If the product you are offering doesn't look exactly like the need as defined, you won't make the finals. There is a class of consultants who will help you get it right. They get paid by institutions to advise on allocations, and design RFPs; but they can be influenced to see the value of your services if you provide research material, free meals, etc. They can help you design the service you have on offer to the criteria of the RFP.

One of the most effective selling tools in the money raising stage is the appearance of alignment of interests. Interests are never completely aligned between an investor and operator (the person or entity that builds and/or manages the product), but you can come close. The investor wants to know that you have skin in the game. The investor will be totally incensed if your fee structure results in a situation where you make money and he/she doesn't. The best fee structure involves a minimum fee up to a level or return that the investor could make on a passive investment and a sliding scale above that. The higher the IRR, the bigger percentage of the return goes to the operator.

Believe it or not, raising money is often the easy part. The hard part is keeping the investor happy and coming back for your next set of deals. That is accomplished by something politely called "portfolio management." Portfolio managers spend their lives reporting to the staff of the institutions from which you got the money. Reporting which is flawless in format, delivered on time, and supplemented by personal attention, will get you more money over time than almost anything else you can do. It is important to produce good returns, but reporting is often at least as important as reality. Institutional investors are anal. The format of the report and its internal consistency are at least important as the financial results. Choose your portfolio managers carefully and reward them handsomely. Get people who will have good chemistry with institutional staffers, and who will do perfect follow-up. Remember that this is a form of selling. Your existing customer is your best source of new money.

In virtually every aspect of every business, your existing customers are the best source of growth and profits.

Portfolio management is not the place for out-of-the-box thinking.

Selling Vacant Space

This is a subject of high emotional content for me. I have never understood industry practice in dealing with vacant space: Leave the existing improvements in place and do a slapdash clean-up. Wait until the new lease is signed before spending any money on the space. To me, that is the equivalent of a clothing retailer displaying dresses that are wrinkled and dirty, in a pile on the floor. Empty space is our product. It deserves to be cleaned, ironed, folded, and sorted by size. Any time I had a project manager or third party property manager who let a space go on the market that did not "shine like a diamond in a goat's ass" I made an immediate change in employment status.

The first issue is the existing tenant improvements. In the great leasing casino of life, the chances that the stuff you put in for the last tenant will be attractive to the next tenant are somewhat longer than Keno or the lottery. It ain't gonna happen. Just because you have a six-fingered glove for rent does not mean you are going to get a six-fingered hand to pay you for it. Tear out all non-generic improvements! If you negotiated your lease properly, your rent stream included the cost of restoring your space to marketable condition. If your industrial building has too much office space, put some of it in the dumpster. Heat, HVAC, heavy power, bathrooms, and some forms of extra lighting, can be left. The rest has to go. Replace the old carpet, or at least tear it up and display bare floor. Nothing turns off a prospective tenant like the smell of dirty carpet. That's not a good first impression to make.

Real estate people who are used to rebuilding space think that a prospective tenant can visualize space as it will look after work is done. NOT SO! Your prospective tenant will see only what you show him/her. Get it as clean and white and as sweet smelling as you can. Put up a large diagram with dimensions (and have paper versions to go). Turn on the heat or AC and lights before a showing. Be sure the bathroom works and there is some toilet paper available.

Most markets for most types of space in the United States are at least a little overbuilt most of the time. That means you are competing for tenants, especially good tenants.

The broker showing your space (and most markets are fully brokered) will be trying to show the prospective tenant every space that even remotely resembles the stated requirement. The fastest way for a broker to lose control is for a competing broker to be able to say to the prospect, "have you seen the space at..." If the answer is no, the competing broker has a chance to get in the deal. All of that means that your space will be one of 5 or 10 or 20 the prospect will see on the tour. On a good day, three of them will be remembered. You want to be first or last. Good broker marketing will get that favor. You want to be the best looking space on the tour. Good space preparation will put you in that position.

8. Lease Documents, Tenant Improvements, Evictions and Bankruptcy

Lease Documents

Most real estate operators make a total hash of this part of the business. If you are signing a 25-year anchor lease in a regional mall, or a lease/option on a high-rise, the lawyer bill you incur may be a good investment. Otherwise, you probably wasted your money. Most leases are five years or less. Many tenants will bail before the 60 months have elapsed. Doing a 50-page agreement to cover such a transaction is a huge waste of money. The reason for a tight legal agreement is to mitigate damages. By the time you get in a fight with the tenant, there isn't enough time left on the lease to generate much of a damage claim on either side.

Think of your lease as a selling tool. Be the path of least resistance. Make it easy for your prospective lessee to do business with you. A simple, straightforward lease document and a dealmaker lawyer will get you more than your share of the business available. You may encounter a tenant's lawyer who wants to take your simple document and mangle it. If you want the tenant badly enough, you'll play. And, if your lawyer is good, the exercise won't cost you anything except legal fees. One way I tried to mitigate that problem when I was doing a lot of industrial leasing was to insist that lease comments be limited to one for every 10,000 feet of leased space. If you were only leasing 10,000 feet, your lawyer had to restrict himself/herself to one comment. If you wanted 10 comments, lease 100,000 feet. I also instructed my attorneys to break off negotiations any time they estimated my total legal bill would be in excess of one month's rent.

There are a few lease sections to which you must pay strict attention. The hazardous materials clause should be iron clad. If the tenant puts something nasty in the ground water under your building, they need to be totally liable to clean it up, and cover all associated damages. If the tenant's operation involves any significant use of hazardous chemicals, there should be some additional security offered to insure the obligation. Also, your bankruptcy provision should be drafted by a lawyer who specializes in bankruptcy. You want to be able to get your space back promptly if the tenant files, and you want to be able to keep the security deposit. A faulty lease document may prevent either or both of those things from happening.

There are a few sections to pay less attention to. Untold millions of dollars have been wasted on Damage and Destruction and Condemnation provisions. Neither is liable to happen. In the event either does happen, the actual event will not have been anticipated by the lease. My only caveat is that you don't warrant that you will rebuild in the event of major damage or destruction. Your insurance company may stiff you or stall. If you don't have insurance proceeds, you don't want to be under legal obligation to rebuild.

It's going to be a beautiful lease. Don't worry about the cost.

Tenant Improvements

Most types of multifamily, industrial, office and retail property are at least a little overbuilt in most parts of the United States most of the time. I remember sitting in an investment committee meeting many years ago when we were considering entering a Canadian market—Toronto, I think. The young guy presenting the proposed investment informed us that the industrial market had never had a vacancy above 5% in living memory. The boss said that, since we and all the other usual American suspects were now entering the market, it would soon be 10%, just like every other market in which we operated. Developers overbuild every chance they get. Even when they see the tsunami of oversupply approaching, they don't stop. At that point, we enter the Lucky Irishman phase. There will soon be way too many buildings, but mine will lease... because mine is prettier and/or because it's ME! More specifically, they have time, money and psychic energy involved in the deal; and don't have enough sense to stop throwing good money after bad.

In a competitive situation, you are almost certainly going to have to modify your vacant space in order to fill the space with paying tenants. When approaching this subject, change hats. You are no longer flogging your product; you are lending money. Think like a banker! Underwrite the credit of the borrower. Underwrite his/her business plan. Get a decent return on investment! Get some security to assure timely repayment.

The prospective tenant and its representative will assure you that their improvement package is their sincere attempt to help you by "improving your building." The best response to that pitch is laughter. Almost nothing you put in for Tenant A will ever be useful to Tenant B. You need to get paid for the improvement over the life of the lease; you need to get a rate of return that exceeds your cost of capital (as all bankers must); and you need to include the cost of removal in your calculation.

When designing a tenant improvement package, be an active participant in the process. Have your space planner do the work. Get the wet walls in the right place. Plan your partial tear-out of excessive office space in advance. If you do this part correctly, you will get some free useful life out of some of the money you spend.

Evictions

Every property owner, but especially anyone owning multifamily, needs a close, personal relationship with an attorney who does evictions. Most major cities have eviction mills. If you run apartments, you will need to choose one. You need someone who is fast and dirty, so that the cost of eviction doesn't eat all your profit. Remember that, generally speaking, apartment owners rent to the lower 1/3 of the socioeconomic ladder. You are going to have people living hand to mouth. Any disruption of income means they can't make the rent. And you need to get the process done correctly. Major cities are full of lawyers trying to get in their pro bono hours who will be happy to stop the process in its tracks over a minor documentary flaw. Eviction laws are fairly uniform, but enforcement is not. In places like NYC, West LA, Santa Monica, and San Francisco, the eviction process is a war. It takes at least 90 days to get a deadbeat out the door, and you will return the security deposit (usually with interest), and you will stipulate that you will not report the default to credit reporting agencies or provide a negative reference to future landlords.

One really effective weapon is the stipulated judgment. The deadbeat tenant will tell the pro bono lawyer that they just need a little time to pay. Pro bono lawyers are stupid enough to believe that sad story. If you can get the commitment memorialized in a stipulated judgment, you can get the sheriff out as soon as there is a failure to perform (which happens in almost every case). Socialist judges and lawyers don't take the agreement you and the tenant signed seriously, but they take agreements they drafted very seriously.

Many jurisdictions go out of their way to sanction landlords for blacklisting deadbeat tenants. That makes it hard to get a genuine reference from a prior or existing landlord. In many cases, the existing landlord will lie in order to get rid of a problem tenant. Be very wary of references. In many jurisdictions there is a convention whereby a landlord will write a very bland and straightforward reference (Mr. and Mrs. Deadbeat were residents from...). That is code for *WATCH YOUR ASS; THESE PEOPLE ARE TROUBLE.*

Many tenants will try to hold out in commercial space by pleading for mercy and/or offering reduced rent. Especially in retail space (where vacant storefronts in a center are a killer) and especially in a soft market, you may be tempted to let a deadbeat stay in occupancy for reduced or nonexistent rent. Resist the temptation! Your product is space. If that space is occupied by someone not paying rent, it is a wasting asset. It is not available to rent to someone who can pay rent. Throw out the deadbeat. Get rid of the inappropriate improvements. Shine it up. Advertise a rent that meets the market. Go forward! The only exception I might make is if the reduced rent approximates the market and you have similar space next door available for immediate occupancy.

Bankruptcy

The other lawyer you'll need to know is one specializing in bankruptcy. Bankruptcy court is a world unto itself, with a subculture all its own. Bankruptcy judges are the closest thing we have to absolute monarchy. They do what they want to do, and there is almost no practical recourse.

Bankruptcy is the heart of the capitalist system. Critics of capitalism think the driving force is self-interest or profit. Wrong. There are many state capitalist enterprises and collusive capitalist enterprises and socialist enterprises that make a profit. The difference between capitalism and socialism is punishment for failure. Socialist enterprises are put out of business only in the most extreme cases, and after all else has failed. A capitalist enterprise has to visit the judge as soon as it is unable to meet payroll. The heart of capitalism is creative destruction. Obsolete products and inept organizations go away, to be replaced by relevant products and efficient organizations. It is not a pretty process, but it really works.

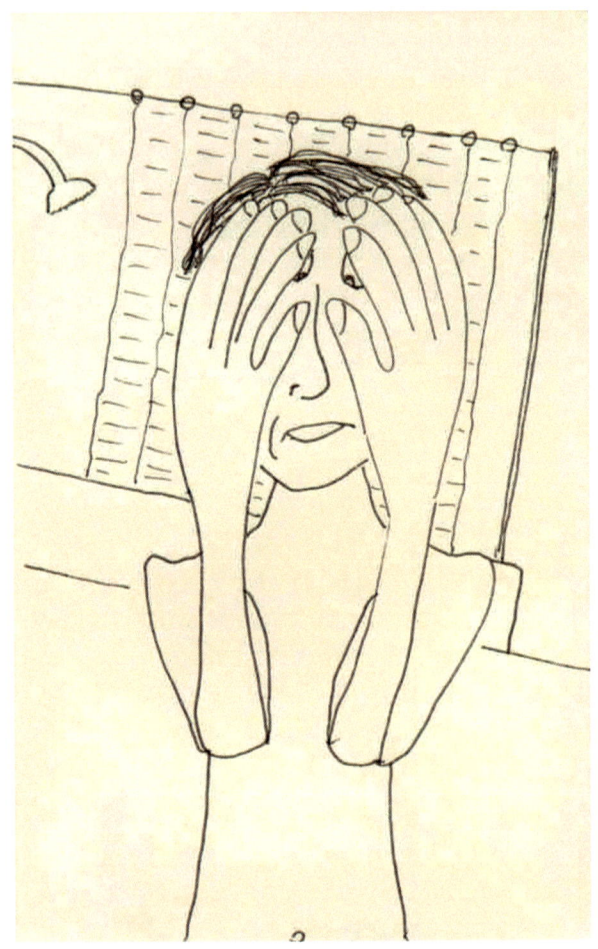

May I finish my shower before you move my belongings out?

The rules of bankruptcy are unlike those of any other court. The judge is king. Your lawyer must be known to the judge and must present a plan the judge likes. If you neglect either of those elements, you will get stiffed.

Retailers are especially fond of bankruptcy. The objective of the average retail chain or franchisor is to open as many outlets as possible as rapidly as possible, in order to grow the company and therefore the compensation of its management. Once the system reaches a certain point, it's time to cull. The method is to assess which stores to keep and which to close; obtain debtor-in-possession financing; walk selected leases in the bankruptcy proceeding; reduce the principal balance of the loan with some creditors; and emerge stronger than ever. One of the reasons the 2008 downturn was so severe was that CIT and GE Capital (the main providers) had to get out of the Debtor In Possession business. Deadbeat retailers had to go Chapter 7 and close all the stores.

As a property owner, you want to be sure you protect your right to get paid or get your space back in a hurry. You want to be able to keep your security deposit (if the lease is improperly drawn, it might be clawed back into the bankruptcy estate). You want to avoid investing money in a chain of retailers. You want to have security outside the lease to recoup tenant improvement expenditure. If you do your job correctly, you can get the lease affirmed or rejected in about 45 days from the filing date. If the lease is affirmed, you will get your money or get your space back moments after any payment deadline has passed. Bankruptcy judges have no patience for sad stories.

One of my claims to fame (or infamy) was that I leased a million plus feet to Webvan—an internet grocery store. The idea was that you would order groceries to be delivered in a fairly tight time frame to your front door. It didn't work. I was stuck with three large warehouses full of conveyors, coolers and freezers. However, I was not a virgin when I did the deals with them. We had an opportunity to lease warehouses all around the country. We decided that three was enough exposure, and confined ourselves to advising them in other locations. We limited the tenant improvement allowance to the amount required to bring in power, install good lighting and build a modest amount of office space and restrooms. We bought buildings for them that were in locations we liked, and had good configuration. I watched them like a hawk.

When they applied for the tenant improvement money for the Washington, DC, unit, I went to see if we got our money's worth of improvements. The contractor installing the freezers had ceased work. I refused to advance the tenant improvement money.

I resent the characterization "fly-by-night."

At that point, we started into the bankruptcy spiral. At the end of the day, we agreed to date certain on the move-out from each location; 150% rent for the period from filing to vacating; complete removal of specialized improvements; and the ability to begin marketing space immediately. Within six months, we had all of the space re-leased, some of it at higher rents. And, we kept our place in the creditor stack, which allowed us to get three distributions from the settlement. In aggregate, we about broke even (if you don't attribute too much compensation for the sleepless nights).

You need to contemplate the possibility of bankruptcy every time you sign a lease. Draft your lease correctly. Know a good bankruptcy lawyer in the jurisdiction of the building and the jurisdiction of the headquarters of the lessee. Get into court within hours of the filing. Enforce every deadline. Negotiate creatively to get your share of the carrion.

My first employer in the warehouse development business went bankrupt in a large cloud of dust. All of the buildings (about 200 of them) were sold to investors and leased back. The court proceeding was a gigantic clusterbleep. I ran 14 of the buildings. The first of my owners to get his building back was finished up in a matter of weeks. His lawyer jumped into a limo with the trustee with an order in hand, which he got signed. It took over two years for the last of my owners to get possession. He had the same building type; the same documentation; the same judge; the same proceeding; but a very different outcome.

9. Real Estate Investment Trusts

You might want to do a little research about the creation of the Real Estate Investment Trust vehicle (REIT). I've read the history on a number of occasions, but most of it slipped out of my mind (due to lack of interest). I'll leave that research to those of you who are interested. The vehicle originated in the 1950s or 60s as a way for the small investor to participate in the ownership of income-producing real estate. There were several fitful starts, but the market never really amounted to much. In the mid-1990s, several significant real estate organizations went public. The main motivation was that the loan markets had frozen up. Going public was a way to cope with the stark fact that loans were not being rolled over at maturity. Raising money from the sale of stock allowed the loans to be retired or reworked. As I recall, Taubman was the bell cow—the leader of the herd. They had high-end malls, which provided a good and coherent story for a Wall Street sales job. Sam Zell went out in a big way with Equity Office (which he sold for a huge number at the top of the market) and Equity Residential. The market sector now had a significant capitalization and appears to be here to stay.

A big problem with REITs is that it is hard to track earnings in a conventional fashion. Almost all of what they own has to be depreciated for accounting purposes on an annual basis. Since accounting depreciation is designed to reflect the deterioration of capital stock (machinery) due to wear, tear and obsolescence, it isn't a good measure to apply to buildings. However, the real estate industry values the concept because it creates tax shelter. REITs do report GAAP EPS (earnings per share), but their primary reporting numbers are Funds From Operations (FFO) and Adjusted Funds From Operations

(AFFO), meaning after capital expenditures. Essentially, FFO is EPS plus the depreciation allowance. If you are going to invest in REIT shares, it is good to study the quarterly filings and listen to the analyst calls until you get onto the lingo.

REIT Investing

We'll apply the same criterion here as we did with negotiation. As opposed to regurgitating easily available information, I'll refer you to a source better than me. If you are going to invest in REIT stock, subscribe to the analyst reports from Green Street. It's expensive, but eminently worth the investment. These folks are smart and numerate and diligent. They have a good conceptual framework for judging pricing of stock and Net Asset Value (NAV). They own no stock, nor do they raise money, which means they have no conflicts of interest. I don't always agree with their valuations, but our disagreements are minor. All of the other analysts I'm aware of work for investment banks, and they definitely have axes to grind. Their employers want to handle follow on stock offerings and bond offerings. They are not going to offend their prospective customers unless they have absolutely no choice.

Advantages of the REIT Model

REITs are not taxed at the corporate level, unlike other publically traded corporations. In order to retain that status, they are obligated to distribute 95% of taxable earnings (that usually works out to about 75% of overall earnings) in the form of dividends. Recipients of the dividend are obligated to pay taxes at the ordinary income level. Some of the dividend might be classed as capital gain, but we won't get that far in the weeds. In general, earnings are taxed once, not twice. All other publically traded corporations are taxed twice—at the corporate level and again at the dividend level. So, let us say a corporation makes a dollar of net profit and doesn't engage in shelter contortions. Thirty five cents of that dollar will have to be paid in taxes. If they pay a dividend of the remaining profit (sixty five cents), and the recipient is a California taxpayer in the top bracket, about thirty cents will go to federal and state taxes (46% of .65). In round numbers, the effective tax take is 64%. With a REIT dividend, total tax take is 46% (50% after the Obamacare tax kicks in).

A note of caution: Be wary of high dividends. Any well run REIT should be retaining as much of its earnings as the law allows to be used to acquire additional properties. A high dividend yield relative to stock price usually means a weak company. The AFFO should be at least 110% of the dividend payout (125% is ideal). If not, the company is wasting assets in order to pay the dividend (selling property or borrowing money).

The second major advantage of the REIT model is liquidity. If you own a building and need to access your equity, you have to list the property; wait for an offer; wait for the buyer to get a loan; pay closing costs; and pay a commission. That's all assuming that you get a buyer at all. There is a limited universe of people with the equity, expertise and horsepower to do a major transaction. If you own a position in a major REIT, you can get cash in 24 hours by calling your broker and telling him/her to sell. A significant percentage of the shares of major companies change hands every day.

Liquidity allows you to engage in strategic timing. If you own a big portfolio of apartments in a place like Denver or Atlanta, and you decide that the supply/demand equation is starting to work against you, you will probably have a hard time liquidating your portfolio before the market starts to hammer your rents and the exit cap rates. There is a continuous change in the relative value of privately and publicly held real estate. You can buy when the public markets are undervaluing real estate, and sell when that anomaly corrects itself. Every product type gets overbuilt periodically. When the number of cranes gets too numerous, it's time to sell your office REIT stock. It typically takes about five years for a badly overbuilt market to regain equilibrium. You can buy three or four years in and get a good value.

A third major advantage is that a well-run REIT has the ability to borrow money in a hurry using its balance sheet. Most people/entities putting a deal together have to get a project-specific loan, which is cumbersome and time consuming. Quality REITs have big credit lines and the ability to float stock and bonds on Wall Street. That gives them a lot of flexibility in buying and selling assets. When investing in a REIT, you should look carefully at the condition of the balance sheet, the level of room to get deals done, and the general level of leverage. My feeling is that 50% leverage is about right. Below that, you are leaving the advantages of leverage on the table (unless effective interest rates exceed free and clear yields). Above that, the stock will get hammered in a downturn of any kind. The Street will conclude that the debt can't be rolled over without major penalties, or that a fire sale of assets will be required.

As the market has evolved, REITs tend to specialize in a specific property type. I exclude from this discussion mortgage REITs (the existence of which I don't really understand). When you buy an REIT stock, you buy a product type, which may be multi-family, office, industrial, hotel, or self-storage. There are even REITs for privately run prisons, nursing homes and trailer parks. My advice is to stick to the basic product types. It's easier to follow the progress of those markets, and the companies that work in those sectors have large float-- there is a significant amount of stock that trades every day. If you own stock in a small-cap, thinly traded entity, you might not be able to sell when you want to, except at a fire sale price.

Our REIT specializes in sports complexes for medium-sized cities.

Some REITs also operate as investment managers. They invest money in their particular property sector on behalf of major institutional players (public and corporate pension plans, sovereign wealth funds, endowments, high net worth individuals). They create funds into which institutional investors can buy units (say, in million dollar increments), which can be cashed in (if funds are available) on a periodic basis (usually quarterly). The investor wishing to withdraw gets in a line, and is paid off on a basis with the first funds available. Shares are valued quarterly based on the appraised value of all the assets in the fund. Some funds have specific time frames and fully liquidate on a date certain (usually there are provisions for extensions up to three years), when all the funds are returned to the investors. In order to create competitive advantage as an investment manager, a REIT will usually invest alongside its investors (10-40% is typical) to create the illusion of alignment of interest. I say illusion because there is hardly ever complete alignment between any manager and its investors. The advantage for the REIT shareholder is that the REIT usually makes a lot of fee income, without having to invest in much overhead to do so. A well run program can put a lot of money on the bottom line. It also allows an REIT to be a much bigger player in a property sector than its own capital and debt would otherwise allow.

The Dark Side

Of course, there are some downsides to the REIT model. Any publically traded vehicle is exposed to all the problems of the regulatory state and the short-term thinking that drives Wall Street. Running a real estate business geared to meeting the quarterly expectations of "The Street" is not ideal. Lots of accounting gyrations and window dressing result from the attempt to meet those expectations. Lots of decisions get made that would not be made by a long-term holder of property. Then, there is Sarbanes Oxley. This legislation was passed as a response to the Enron scandal. The Enron guys committed fraud.

We didn't need another law. The new law imposes redundant processes that allow audit firms to charge a lot more for their certification of financial statements of publically traded companies. A gigantic waste of money. The average large REIT wastes up to $2,000,000 per year in a useless compliance process. A much better use of money would be aggressive enforcement of the fraud statutes already on the books before SOX was conceived.

There are, of course, real instances of questionable and fraudulent behavior. Some CEOs have set up companies they own, which provide services to their REIT at prices that don't pass the giggle test. Some REITs have shareholder structures that give insiders much more power than they should have. However, I suspect that the level of fraud and financial gimmickry is no higher in REIT-land than other lines of business.

For damn sure, most REITs have more overhead than a well-run privately held entity owning the same real estate. Development or investment organizations tend to compensate based on results. They stay pretty lean because the principals are taking the profit home. In a REIT structure, there is a lot less pressure to stay lean. As with all bureaucracies, payday comes every two weeks no matter how the property is performing. The pressures of regulatory requirements, tax reporting, investor reporting, analyst massaging, etc. generate a lot of hiring of expensive and bureaucratically minded people. When investing in a REIT, look carefully at the ratio of overhead to income.

Finally, there is the temptation for REIT CEOs to play developer. Some do it pretty well because they were developers who had to go public in order to roll over debt. They are generally better at developing than running a publicly traded vehicle. Some do it pretty well because they develop very selectively, usually to enhance existing assets. Federal Realty buys clusters of retail buildings in upscale suburban downtowns. They have successfully redeveloped to upgrade the neighborhood and added some mixed-use elements to their clusters with great success. One major REIT, which shall go unnamed for these purposes, had such a load of development volume in 2008 that they came inches from a visit to the Bankruptcy Court. Development is not a programmatic business; it should be an opportunistic business. The time and place have to be right. It's almost impossible to make money on new construction in a falling market. When rents are deteriorating, smart developers shut the door. It's a good time to travel to places they've never been and/or lower their handicap. A REIT pursuing a development program will have a volume goal, and will have communicated earnings expectations to The Street. It's hard to shut that sort of thing down. There is also the evil temptation to accumulate a land bank. Having land at a good basis can generate great development profits, but owning land in a down market is the equivalent of swimming while towing an anchor. In a down market, land is worth less than nothing (you can't sell it or finance it, and you still have to pay taxes and insurance). Smart developers buy a little land for cash in soft markets, and plan to keep it until such time as it pays to build. The emphasis should be on "little" and "cash."

Private REITs and Tenants In Common (TICs)

Neither of these vehicles belongs in the same chapter as real REITs, but I have no other logical place to talk about these abominations, and the warning needs to be passed along.

A so-called private or non-traded REIT is syndication by another name. Here's a typical deal: A financial advisor is paid about 6 cents on the dollar to raise money from naïve clients searching for return in a return-starved market. The archetypical sucker is a retired person looking for income on which to live. The advisor sends the money to the sponsor, who promptly takes another 10 cents or so off the top. The remaining 84 cents is invested in a buildings leased for a long term to a creditworthy tenants. The return on the 84 cents, less a management fee, is paid to the investor. There is a promise of future liquidity, because the entity is set up to be taken public. In some cases, these entities have actually gone public, in which case the price of the publically traded stock tends to be about 50% of the price for which the units were originally sold. *BEWARE! STAY AWAY! DON'T GET SUCKED IN!*

The big trap is the allure of steady income from creditworthy tenants. A promise that is fulfilled in the early stages of the deal. A big corporation has sold its building to a sponsor at a great price, with a healthy lease-back rent. The seller gets the liquidity, can get the depreciation off its balance sheet, and keeps good control of the building by means of a long lease and lots of options. The problem is that the facility is usually useless or semi-useless when the lease ends. It was built by a user, for its needs, in a location that suited those needs. The improvement probably has little appeal to any other users. Assuming that the improvements have some appeal, getting a new tenant will require marketing skills, a lot of time, and money to pay for alterations and commissions. There is no infrastructure in the average private REIT organization to do any of this. No money was set aside to meet debt service during the period of vacancy or pay for the turnover costs. The whole damn thing blows up at the end of the lease term. *STAY AWAY!*

TICs are even worse. The structure consists of a group of strangers entering into an agreement to own a piece of income property together. A sponsor has arranged for the purchase and management of the asset, and takes a generous fee for his/her efforts. Why would any investor agree to such irrationality? As with all scams, the answer is: greed. The investors are usually people who have sold investments and don't have enough money and/or expertise and/or willingness to execute a 1031 exchange (capital gains tax is deferred if you trade one real estate asset for another) on their own. But, they are facing a large tax bill, which they don't want to pay. Most of the tax is actually a tax on a tax, because a large part of the gain is inflation (inflation being a tax on wealth imposed by government without the grief involved in passing a law). Investing in a TIC defers the tax bite. Somebody else does the 1031 on your behalf. All that is good; and the return might even be decent. The problem arises when the building needs a new roof, or the tenant goes broke, or the sponsor goes over the mountain, or one of the people in the investor group gets into a messy divorce. Then, you have a gaggle of partners you've never met, most of whom will be unable to agree on anything—especially if it involves reaching into their pockets. *STAY THE HELL AWAY!*

10. Entitlements

In My Opinion

This might be entitled the In My Opinion chapter. You're going to get a lot of opinions, mostly of the cynical and negative variety.

Before I start this screed, a large caveat is in order. Most of the negative things I have to say apply to large jurisdictions. Small towns and suburban communities have planning commissioners and city council persons who work for little or no pay and are very public spirited. You can encounter the occasional ideologue, but most of the people involved are quite reasonable. There may be some inefficiencies and some planning staffers can highjack the process, but that is the exception, not the rule. Larger cities and wealthy enclaves are the trouble spots.

In my opinion, government regulation, at most levels of government, has run off the tracks. Look at some of the sectors where the government in one way or another exercises great control--education, mail delivery, energy production and distribution, land use, health care, finance (especially finance of housing). Notice any pattern? The problem is that government is doing the wrong thing. I am not advocating some libertarian fantasy. Regulation is an absolutely essential part of a well-functioning economy. But today's government isn't really regulating; it's participating. Instead of being a referee enforcing a level playing field, and punishing fraudulent behavior, government is a major player. Sometimes the government is the quarterback. That's why there are over 30,000 registered lobbyists in Washington and probably more than 30,000 not registered. There are thousands more in state capitals and major cities. Participants in the economy are paying protection to--and seeking advantage from--the Leviathan.

With respect to land use, the problem is particularly pernicious. Democracy is a great form of government, but it doesn't work well without citizen participation and complete transparency. Land use is an area of regulation well below the radar. With respect to most any site within 100 miles of the Atlantic or Pacific coast, and in many large cities in between, land use regulation is corrupt at its core. Proceedings of the local Design Review Board (or its equivalent) aren't democratic. There is inside baseball when it comes to appointing members of the Board. Nobody shows up at the hearings except interested parties and the occasional gadfly. The results aren't on the evening news, except in very rare and controversial instances. If reporters do show up, the real work doesn't get done until 2:00 AM, when they have all given up and gone home. The entire process renders real estate development, and the resulting levels of rents and sale prices much higher than they would otherwise be.

My partners and I recently built a condo project in a major American city. The aggregate load of governmental extractions for each of the units was $110,000. That is to say, before the buyers bought any walls and fixtures, they paid $110,000 for impact fees, lobbyists, lawyers, a percentage of the units that had to be sold below cost, street improvements, etc. The process from start to finish was 8 years. You would be hard pressed to come up with a more inefficient way of producing shelter. And the same people who complain most loudly about the lack of affordable housing imposed all of those costs. The net effect of current land use regulation is to increase the cost of all structures to be built. The poor get screwed, because they get priced out. In order to make up for that unintended consequence, fees for low-income housing are heaped onto the load, transferring the cost to market rate buyers and renters. A lucky few low-income people (those picked in the lottery) get subsidized housing; everybody else gets screwed. A gigantic hidden tax! But the fees heaped on new development don't show. It appears that the jurisdiction is covering its cost of producing subsidized housing, without resorting to the unpleasant alternative of taxing its constituents. Very few of those constituents will figure out that the taxes are being passed along to them in the form of higher prices and higher rents.

The whole process is tilted toward NO. Any reasonably well organized group of NIMBYs or BANANAs (Build Absolutely Nothing Anywhere Near Anything) can hire a lawyer and stall any proposed development for years. Odds are they can wear out the average developer; or get the proposal turned down entirely; or get the proposed development cut back to the point of unprofitability. In California, the easiest hook is the EIR (Environmental Impact Report). An EIR is a lengthy document that is supposed to inform any public official voting on the proposed development to be fully informed of all possible environmental impacts and alternate uses of the site. Costs of $100,000 are not unusual. The public authority picks the vendor; the aspiring developer pays the cost. The opponents will take a small project (which is usually exempted from the requirement due to size) before a judge with the argument that an EIR needs to be done. Most judges figure the path of least resistance is to say yes. In that instance, the developer is obligated to pay the legal fees of both sides. If there is an appeal, the developer appealing must post a large bond; the NIMBY appealing can do so for free.

Finally, you need to know, with total certainty, that you as a property owner have no rights. That portion of the Fifth Amendment specifying compensation for taking of property by government entities has long since been rendered ineffective by various court decisions. You will do what the City Council or Design Review Board, of Board of Supervisors or Planning Commission tells you to do. In a very few instances, I have known developers who were treated so shoddily and arbitrarily that they sued and won. In two instances of which I'm aware, small cities were effectively driven to the wall financially. However, you have to have truly egregious behavior by a government entity, a very deep pocket, very steady nerves, a very good lawyer, and a lot of patience to win.

If you are going to build or own commercial property, you are going to deal with the regulatory climate. I'll try to give you a few useful tips for dealing with the beast.

First, a shortcut. There was a wonderful woman named Debra Heller Stein. She was taken much before her time, but she left a great legacy. She published a great deal of material on the subject of entitlements, which I recommend that you read before trying to build anything in coastal America. Her basic message is that every deal is a political war, which requires you to find political allies before you wade onto the battlefield. Find all the groups who will benefit from your project. Make contributions to a non-profit or church who can be induced to support you. Create your own crowd for the hearing. Get your own set of letters and petitions. Fight fire with fire! Debra was the master. Learn from the master.

Your first job as an aspiring developer, or financier backing a developer, is to see if the stars are aligned. No matter how much money you are willing to spend; no matter how astute your political and public relations effort; no matter how smooth your tongue; you aren't going to build a Wal-Mart in Santa Monica or Bethesda. You need to troll around and read the rules and talk to a few of the connected folks in the community to see if there is any light at the end of the tunnel. You need to look at the market for your deal or get a commitment from a user. You need to assess the loan market and construction costs, to be sure there is margin in your deal. Then, you need to go back and rerun the numbers with a significant contingency if you are going to face political opposition. In coastal America, it will take more time and cost more money than you think. If it looks like you are about to wade into a swamp with a bottom you can't easily identify, go elsewhere!

Your next job is to learn how the game is played in the jurisdiction in which you intend to build. Every jurisdiction has a lot of unwritten rules that are in a constant state of flux. To certain players, homage must be paid. Intractable opponents must be mollified. The Council may follow the recommendations of the Planning Commission slavishly; or they may automatically reverse anything that comes up on appeal. The Planning Director may be respected or ignored. Some jurisdictions will approve a local developer and tank any foreigner. You may need a local partner in order to get to yes. If you're going to play the game, get to know the rules, most of which are not written down anywhere.

Your most important job is to find and retain the services of the best fixer in town. It might be a lawyer; it might be a retired mayor; it might be a civil engineer; it might be a land use consultant; it might be a combination of some of the above. Attend a few meetings of the Council and Commission. See who likes whom. See whose deals are getting approved. Watch the body language. Talk to the planners to see whose opinions they respect. You need to build a team that is as local and credible as possible. If you arrive at the hearing with a pack of strangers, you will either lose, or your project will get modified in a very expensive fashion.

Be fully aware that your political team members will not really be working for you, even though you will be paying the bill. In some cases, there are professional standards that must be respected. You can't ask a member of a profession to damage his/her reputation in service of your project. More importantly, your fixers have to live in the community long after you're gone. Their value is their relationship with the bureaucrats and politicians. They have to guard those relationships very carefully. Preserving standards and relationships may cost you some money, but that is a price you will have to pay to get your deal done. If your deal can't stand the cost, the stars aren't aligned.

Once you have put your team together and gathered your allies, you need to hustle everybody in the process. Meet with every planning commissioner and every member of the council. It is most important to meet with those who oppose the project, and go out of your way to respect their objections. It is important that the "no" vote doesn't come with baggage. Many "no" votes mean that the commissioner doesn't like the project or wants to stay straight with his/her constituency. A vehement "no" vote often means that friends on the council or commission are being asked to vote "no" in solidarity. Political capital is being spent. If you have spent your time properly, you can turn a vehement "no" into a simple "no" that won't drag any other votes along. In some cases, you may have more than enough votes, but some of your "yes" votes would be better off politically to vote "no." Turn them loose. You are trying to make as many friends as possible. You are searching for the path of least resistance. Leave the hearing with as many people in the room feeling good as possible. Tell everybody that they beat your brains out, but you're proud and happy to be a good corporate citizen of their community. Never pick a fight you don't have to pick. Remember that there is some valid basis for land use regulation. Your structure will be there long after you've gone over the hill. The people who have to live with it in the long run deserve a voice in its design. Respect that legitimate concern.

Two final pieces of land use advice. Never, ever, ever, ever, ever close on the land until you have a permit. We're back to the negotiating chapter. As long as you haven't closed, you have a hostage. If the regulatory burden gets too heavy, you can walk away. Once you close, your hostage is gone. Unless you want to eat the whole cost of the land, you will end up doing whatever you are told, even if it means losing money.

Second, politics costs money. I am not talking about corruption or pay to play (although that has been known to go on). I am talking about making selective political contributions at appropriate times, sponsoring a hole at the Planning Commission golf tournament, buying some dinners, hiring some local vendors, etc. If you cheap this part out, you won't get your deal approved. People can't run for office without money. A little generosity can go a long way. A little stinginess will get you an ass kicking.

11. Land

Now that we've discussed the generalities of the real estate business (with stunning superficiality and no footnotes whatever), I'll move briskly to specifics.

BEWARE!

Mark Twain is supposed to have said: "Buy land; they're not making any more of it." Turns out that was bad advice. Governmental entities and environmental activists are working day and night to move more and more land from private to public ownership. They are calling it a Public Trust or Wilderness or some other worthy sounding nonsense. If you think this will work out well in the long run, take a look at your neighborhood public housing project. In my opinion, if everybody owns it, nobody takes care of it.

In addition to outright seizure, planning authorities and NIMBY activists are working overtime to restrict the uses to which property owners may put their land. In the case of the California Coastal Commission, owners of land adjoining the Pacific Ocean have an absolute right to allow unlimited public access to the water across their land, and no right to any other use. You can't remodel your kitchen without their permission (which will include additional extractions).

The conclusion is that you don't want to own land. You want to own the right to use land. Never invest in land of any kind until you have your legal ducks completely in a row.

Secondly, you should avoid leverage. Unless you have your land leased on a long-term basis, under a tight contract, to a very creditworthy lessee, any debt is very dangerous. The land market rises and falls very rapidly depending upon conditions in the market for the product most suited to the land in question (or the use for which it is zoned). If the market for product is soft, the market for land is non-existent. I have endured several significant periods in which land was worse than worthless.

I own several pieces of land with some partners. I'm very happy to have the land and consider the pieces valuable assets. However, they are fully entitled; they are free of debt; and there is no time horizon on the investment. We are prepared to sell, lease, or build-to-suit (for sale or lease) whenever we get an offer we consider attractive. In the meantime, no debt clock is ticking.

Some of the smartest developers I know actively speculate in land. They buy land for cash (after obtaining bullet proof development agreements) from developers who are in trouble, or lenders who have foreclosed, when the market is on its ass. In the early 90s, it was possible to buy fully improved residential subdivisions and industrial parks for less than the cost of the infrastructure and permits. Significant fortunes were made by those with cash.

I was once quoting a build-to-suit deal on a long held piece of dirt. In order to get the deal, I brought the dirt into the calculation at cost. I was asked by a well-meaning critic what the dirt would sell for on the open market; and then asked to compare my pro forma profit on the build-to-suit with the profit I could make selling the land at current market. Turns out the numbers were about the same. All of my projected profit in the build-to-suit was just land mark-up. I was then asked why I wanted to go to all the trouble and risk of doing the build-to-suit when I could make the same money just selling the land. Good question. I've never forgotten it.

Agricultural Land

The median projection from the United Nations (in my opinion, coming from one of the few branches of the UN that isn't a corrupt waste of the 20% of its expenses borne by the American taxpayer) is that world population will top out at 9 billion about 2050. That means a lot more mouths to feed. On current trend, those mouths will eat more per capita. Despite the best efforts of nanny government in Europe and America to strangle enterprise with regulation; and despite the failure of China and India to proceed briskly down the path of liberalization; the magic of markets and innovation is generating greater prosperity. Even sub-Saharan Africa seems to be getting on board. Prosperous people consume more calories. And more of the calories they consume come from meat, which requires more agricultural input per calorie.

More mouths to feed means prosperity for American agriculture, a sector of the economy which is marvelously productive. The following numbers aren't exactly correct, but close. In 1800, about 75% of the population was engaged in food production. Today, it's less than 1%. Agriculture has produced more gains in productivity than most any other sector of the economy. And they've done it on less land. The Great Plains is becoming plains again because marginal land in the Dakotas is being abandoned, and is reverting to its pre-cultivation state. In due course, the buffalo will roam again.

All of that makes farmland progressively more valuable. And it is a fit investment class. A great deal of farmed land is not owned by the guy sitting on the tractor (in air-conditioned comfort following GPS instructions). Many farms are leased to operators for fixed or percentage rents. Many of the lessors are retired farmers, but many are also absentee investors. It's a good business if you buy at the right time and do proper research. You need to understand soil chemistry, crop yields, commodity markets, hydrology, and the current and probable future state of government intervention (price supports, crop insurance, etc.). You also need to be sure that your farmer does not exhaust the land by failure to rotate corps; application of inadequate fertilizer; and/or destructive plowing procedures. If you are prepared to make that investment in research and management, there is money to be made owning farmland.

A variation is timberland. Wood is an excellent and valuable renewable resource. Sadly, environmentalists (in my opinion) have turned the business into a nightmare of litigation. In service of the spotted owl, the American timber/lumber industry has been seriously wounded and hundreds of thousands of loggers and mill workers have been told that their economic future should be eco-tourism. My favorite retort is a bumper sticker often seen in logging country: "Wipe your ass with a spotted owl." Having said all that, selective investment in stands of timber which can legally be cut, and which is properly managed for reproduction, can be a real moneymaker. I would not, however, invest a dime without a lot of research. With respect to the timber business, the regulatory climate is a real jungle.

Development Dirt

The current fad in planning is density. The catch phrase is "transit oriented growth." We are all supposed to live in high-rise buildings next to public transit, and recreate in urban parks. The only problem the planners have is that, in great part, the public ain't buyin' it. Meaning that more green field sites will continue to be developed, at least in the United States, and for the foreseeable future. Our population is still growing. Unlike Europe, Japan and Russia, we have a positive demographic (at least we did until this last recession). The population is aging, but not in a terminal fashion. Our population is also moving. In general, the North and East are losing people and the South and West are gaining. Those dynamics create demand for stores, housing, warehouses, etc. In order to accommodate those needs, raw land will need to be entitled and supplied with infrastructure (streets, curbs, gutters, sidewalks, utility hookups, storm drainage, streetlights, etc.). There is a great deal of money to be made by those who engage in land development, but also a great deal of money to be lost. A successful land developer must have excellent political instincts, good legal help, a lot of patience and patient capital. The process can take a long time. No one should undertake the process that doesn't have the time and the money.

The most obvious area of land development is single-family subdivisions. Lots are usually sold to builders in batches. Sometimes, the entire subdivision is sold to a builder as paper lots (entitled, but not improved) or finished lots. Improvements are often funded by bonds, which are serviced as a part of property taxes paid by the ultimate homeowner. Floating such bond issues is a field unto itself. Get the right lawyer and he/she will lead you through the process. You should not hire Hillary Clinton. Her subdivision bond efforts in Arkansas didn't work out all that well.

In addition to the timing issues involved in getting lots fully entitled and served by utilities, there is the issue of the volatility of the housing market. When interest rates are high, or after a spasm of overbuilding due to artificially low interest rates (2007-2012), the market for newly constructed homes can disappear. A successful land developer must be able to ride out the bad patches by holding his/her product off the market.

I have done a few medium sized (50-100 acres) industrial parks in my time. I did not sell the lots for the most part; I built out the parks. The rules of thumb that I developed as a result of those (sometimes painful) experiences are as follows:

- The finished dirt should be worth at least twice the cost of raw dirt.
- Take your projected time line and multiply by 2.
- Be sure that your first phase of buildings has enough margin to cover the cost of the entire infrastructure and the remaining dirt.

12. Single Family

Homes for Rent

A few years ago, I would not have included a chapter on this subject. It was a mom-and-pop business. Small time investors would own a house or two, almost always in marginal neighborhoods, as part of a retirement or savings program. Due to the great 2007 meltdown, that has changed. Rental housing has become a big business. I was recently at a conference listening to a guy who said he was buying nine houses a day. Hundreds of millions of dollars are flooding into the space. Foreclosure and tax sales used to attract a few bidders who tended to collude with each other (decide in advance who would be the successful bidder and arrange payoffs to the others). No more. Wall Street money and private equity funds are now in the game. The government spent years impeding the market clearing process to little avail; rationality is now starting to prevail. So-called mortgage relief gave money to a few struggling house dwellers (they weren't owners because their loan exceeded the value of their house), but the rest of us were robbed in the process. The futility of that approach seems to have become obvious to almost all participants in the process at this point. Current efforts are focused on allowing those whose loans are close to being in balance to refinance at today's (government induced) low rates.

If you are interested in finding out how this mess evolved, read Gretchen Morgenson's "Reckless Endangerment." She lays it out and names names. Certainly, there are a lot of culprits. Borrowers who signed fraudulent loan applications; mortgage brokers who showed them how to do it; Wall Street houses that bundled wads of crap loans;

rating agencies that blessed the crap; and greedy investors who thought they could get outsized returns by hiding behind AAA ratings. However, none of it would have been possible without FANNIE and FREDDIE there to provide the backstop. In the game of hot potato, somebody is at the end of the line. The Government Sponsored Entities raised money in the public marketplace at very low rates due to the implied backing of the US Treasury (which backing went from implied to explicit when they were nationalized) and lent the money to subprime borrowers. They booked a fat spread (which was a theoretical spread, because the borrowers ended up not paying) and paid themselves handsomely for their fine work. Johnson and Raines, the two CEOs who drove FANNIE into the ditch, made hundreds of millions. The taxpayers ended up with the hot potato. In my opinion, you can properly analyze such scandals by looking for the troughs instead of focusing on the pigs. Human nature is human nature; pigs will always be with us. Government finds some suffering it proposes to alleviate, which will make all those doling out other people's money feel good about themselves. It proceeds to build a trough, which creates a fierce constituency for the continued existence of the trough. When it all goes wrong, a jihad against the pigs is declared. Government provided the credibility for the GSEs to borrow cheaply and it provided the imprimatur that underpins the rating agencies. Without that support, the liar borrowers, sleazy loan brokers, fly by night packagers, etc., would not have been able to access the money.

The interesting question remaining is how well the market clearance process will work on the ground. Managing rent houses is not the same as managing apartments. You can't just hire an on-site manager; connect him/her to an accounting system; and hire or contract for maintenance and unit turnover. It's going to take a lot more organizational sophistication to run hundreds or thousands of houses scattered over a wide area. In an era where lots of skilled tradesmen need work, and lots of mobile technology is available, it seems possible; but it won't be easy.

As far as the individual investor or small syndicate goes, there is still room. I believe the way to analyze a market is to go back 20 years or so and look at pricing in a neighborhood. Prices generally move with inflation (or just a bit more due to supply constraints imposed by governmental entities). Look at house prices in the neighborhood as of 20 years ago and escalate by inflation. That will set a base replacement value. If you can buy a house for a price that fully accounts for deferred maintenance, and is priced below the long-term price trend, there is money to be made. Hold it for a few years; do a "for sale" remodel (paint, landscape and maybe a kitchen); and you should be able to move it for a good gain. In order to compete with the big dogs, you should specialize in a few select neighborhoods and become a real expert. That will allow you to outbid them and still make good money. If you look at markets from the most expensive to the cheapest (Beverly Hills to Victorville), my selection would be somewhere in the middle. The most expensive markets hardly ever get cheap enough to justify speculative buying; the cheapest markets should probably never have been built in the first place, and may never come back.

One way to maximize your profit in rent housing is to manage aggressively. Spend some time underwriting your tenants. There are services available that will tell you virtually everything there is to know about a prospective tenant. Your best tenant may be the former owner of the house, who could not afford debt service, but may be able to afford rent. Once you have selected a tenant, negotiate a rental agreement that incentivizes him/her to take good care of the house. A tenant who will water and mow, make minor repairs, etc., will be worth looking for and rewarding. One obvious incentive is an option the buy the house (which needs to contain a cost of living provision). You should also stay on top of maintenance issues (termites, roof condition, sewer/septic systems). You want your neighborhood to stay maintained, and you don't want to be looking at expensive cures to deferred maintenance when it comes time to sell.

House Flipping

This is a fad that comes along every now and again. Word gets out that home prices only go up. The path to quick riches is to buy a beat up house in a decent neighborhood; fix it up; and sell for a big profit. I've actually done a little of this business and made a little money. However, there are some pitfalls. Prices can go down. The buying frenzy usually occurs just before that phenomenon sets in. In my first try as a house flipper, we had a perfectly good house in a perfectly good neighborhood at a really good price (because it came out of an estate and was truly beat up). We did a good job of remodeling (far more than we should have). When it came time to sell, interest rates had spiked to 9%. We had a short-term carryback from the estate, and were not sophisticated enough to renegotiate with the lien holder. We sold against a deadline and got our ass kicked. We barely made wages. I learned a lot about deadlines. All of my short-term loans now have extension options built in. If we had been able to hold the house for another year, or had enough horsepower to carry our own paper, we would have made good money.

The important thing to know about house flipping is that the profits are mostly an illusion. The people who buy and flip houses are usually convinced that it is their shrewd eye for a bargain, and their expertise at construction management and decorating, that creates the profit. In most cases, it is a rising market.

Many years ago, when I was a graduate student, I read a lot of works by John Kenneth Galbraith. He was an agricultural economist, a flaming socialist, and the pet economist of the Kennedy family. Most of what he wrote was nonsense, but he was au courant reading for anyone studying politics or economics. One thing he wrote has stuck with me all these years. He defined financial genius as a short memory in a rising market. A successful house flipper is usually a financial genius. He/she would have been even smarter to just buy the house and sit on it for a few months. Saves all that time and money invested in the remodeling process.

13. Apartments

Getting Started

My first experience as a landlord came in 1964 when I inherited a little duplex in Corning, California. As I remember, each of the units rented for $75/month. I sold it to a local investor and carried back a first (there were virtually no lenders for little multi-family deals in those days, especially in markets like Corning). I eventually discounted the first by 20%, and used it as a down payment on a three-flat building in the Mission district of San Francisco. My wife and son and I still own that building. When I bought the building, our family lived in the lower unit (the upper units brought in better rent). Our friends were afraid to come across Market Street. It was a fairly safe neighborhood, but filled with recent immigrants from the Philippines, Mexico and Central America. Now it is filled with cutting edge tech types.

I have always believed that apartments are a great core investment. My basic retirement planning revolved around owning free and clear multifamily property. That's not universal advice. When dealing with flat spots (places that are geographically and politically flat)--Phoenix, Denver, Atlanta, Houston, Dallas—be wary. Those markets get severely overbuilt on a regular basis. You can make money buying at or near the bottom, but you need to sell in time, or have the horsepower to ride out the storms. In supply constrained markets, apartments are good year in and year out. Unlike other forms of commercial real estate, you can always rent them. You may have to cut your rents a bit and tolerate a bit or turnover and vacancy, but you can always make enough to cover debt service if you put up a decent (20% or more) down payment (40% in flat spot markets) when you bought them. Thanks to irrational government policy, you can get fixed rate, long-term loans. That's a huge bargain in a world that will almost certainly see a lot of inflation in the mid- to long-term. The world's advanced economies have all taken on huge debts, and made promises that will generate much more debt. The path of least resistance in the face of unpalatable debt has, throughout history, been to devalue the debt thru inflation. If you own an asset whose debt will be amortized reliably by the tenants, whose rent you can raise on a regular basis to keep up with inflation; and that you can eventually own free and clear just by making your debt service every month--you will be hard pressed to find a more reliable method of accumulating wealth.

Management is the Key to Success.

Unfortunately, getting management right is hard to do, because it takes two entirely different personalities to get it done right. A good manager views an apartment building in a motherly fashion. The buildings and the tenants are treated somewhat like children. A good manager actually likes interaction with tenants, and is interested in their welfare. Well-managed buildings tend to have less turnover and less bad behavior because mother is watching. A good manager regards every leak or bit of graffiti as a personal insult.

However, the other key to profitability is watching every penny. When I was about 10, I had a paper route in western Los Angeles (we lived in a pretty affluent neighborhood, even though mom and I were periodically on welfare). My compensation consisted of a percentage of the subscription revenue. I had to collect from about a hundred subscribers. My pay was the last 15 or so. You would be amazed at what lengths people will go to get a paper for free. Pretending not to be home was at the top of the list. I had to go by at odd hours to ambush them. I DID GET MY MONEY, but it wasn't ever easy. The system was unfair to the carriers, but it taught me a great lesson. As a developer or property owner, I get the last dime. The lender gets paid; the county gets its property tax; the roof gets replaced; the insurance company gets its money. If there is anything left over, I get "spendable" return. A concept that is quite antique in today's IRR driven world, but one I hang on to. So, every apartment owner needs a penny pincher in the equation. It either takes two people of different personalities to run a building or somebody who can give himself a regular personality transplant.

Once you get enough units, you can apply both talents to your business. In the beginning, it's a balancing act. The big mistake is to get the roles out of line. Lots of investors love to wallow in numbers. They hire managers who will produce numbers and pinch pennies on command. The net effect is a lot of pissed off tenants. Only in the real estate business could we go out of our way to alienate our customers and call it success.

The Cold, Hard Facts of Life

In general, two thirds of households in America live in an owner-occupied single-family dwelling. The remaining one third of households live in an apartment. In general, apartment dwellers are the bottom third of the socio-economic pecking order. There is a minor market of rentals for affluent people, but I have always stayed out of it, because the customer base is so thin. There are a lot of affluent renters in cities with rent control, because renting is heavily subsidized by governmental fiat. As the Wall Street Journal once said, rent control is the second most effective way to destroy a city; carpet-bombing is the

I feel terrible about that leak. I'll get you a piece of gum for it.

most effective. However, it is a winning strategy for buying votes. Politicians can pretend they are defending the helpless renters from the rapacious landlords. In fact, they are stealing from one middle class group (property owners) and giving the money to another middle class group (renters who work the system). Any property owner renting a rent-controlled unit will pick the most prosperous applicant, of whom there will be many.

The moral of the story for apartment builders or investors is that you are mostly dealing with poor people. Some of your tenants are only temporarily poor. Immigrants gaining language and job skills and new entrants to the work force will move on once they earn enough for a house. The rest of your tenant base will rent for life, because they will never accumulate enough money to buy a house (now that the 20% down payment has made a comeback). A lot of these people were seduced into home ownership in the early 2000s with liar loans, but they're all back in the renter pool by now.

What makes people poor? The bleeding hearts will tell you that it's bad luck, oppression, etc. My experience (of which I have a great deal) does not comport with that view. Most poor people lack education and critical thinking skills because they dropped out of school. Almost all of them do not grasp the concept of deferred gratification. They will seek today's pleasure without consideration of the pain it may bring tomorrow. When the pain arrives, they are almost always surprised. A very significant segment of the poor are abusing alcohol and/or other mood altering chemicals. About 15% of the population is on something. Most of them are poor or end up poor. I'm not being uppity here. I used to abuse alcohol myself. Most important for you as a landlord, they have no financial reserves. Any setback leaves them unable to pay rent.

Those of you who disagree with my analysis will say that low IQ, improper upbringing, mental illness, etc., are the cause of the problem. I know a lot of people who aren't all that smart, who were raised in horrendous environments, who have emotional problems, and who are former drinkers/users. Many of them are able to grasp deferred gratification and get to the stage of home ownership. America really is a place where hard work and frugality are rewarded. Some apartment dwellers work hard, but, aside from those just passing thru, most aren't frugal.

The other cold, hard fact of life is that rent collection is a war in many jurisdictions. Most big cities in America are governed by people whose political philosophy is left of center. They regard renters as victims and property owners as oppressors. Most large law firms demand that their junior associates engage in pro bono work. The partners think that helps them recruit better lawyers; that it burnishes their credentials; and that it provides learning experiences they don't have to bill to their clients. The average eviction court is a rats' nest of trolling lawyers looking to come to the rescue of your deadbeat tenant. In some cases, the government actually pays for tenant advocates.

How do you cope with this nonsense? First, you remember that you have the resolve to get to the end of the battle. The other team does not. If your deadbeat had the horsepower to win, he/she would not have been behind in the rent to begin with. A good eviction lawyer will beat a fresh-faced law school punk every time, IQ differential notwithstanding.

Second, spend the time and money to properly qualify your tenants. In this age of zero privacy, the expenditure of a few bucks will buy you a service that gives you credit history, criminal history, etc. Be careful to whom you rent. It's a good idea to check with prior landlords, but you have to decipher responses. Many property owners you talk to are trying to get rid of a bad tenant by sending them along to you. Go one landlord further back. Some are afraid of being sued. There is a protocol. If you are getting a bland report that mostly consists of occupancy dates, the message being conveyed is WATCH YOUR ASS! Check employment. If I am renting in the Peoples' Republic of San Francisco (where it is very hard to evict), I am looking for employment longevity and security. In addition to talking to a supervisor, I often go to the place of business to be sure it exists, and is viable. If possible, I talk to somebody who isn't the prospective tenant's supervisor to get a second opinion.

Third, get your paperwork in order. The first line of defense for the young lawyer (aka poverty pimp) is to assert that your filing is technically defective. You can save yourself a lot of money by doing a lot of the preliminary eviction work yourself, but you must dot all of the i's. Your lease document needs to be totally up to snuff with respect to contemporary law and practice in your jurisdiction. Your service needs to be letter perfect. If you are evicting for bad behavior, you need to be thoroughly documented. Third party statements (from other tenants) and security camera footage are the most effective weapons. When you get to the mediation phase, the tenant will promise perfect behavior in future and the judge may buy it. At that point, you get a stipulated judgment detailing the promised performance. When that performance isn't forthcoming (and it never is), you now have an effective club with which to beat the judge and pro bono lawyers into submission.

As you can see, I am a tad emotional on this subject, but a great deal of experience will do that for you.

Fourth, get a good eviction lawyer. Every major city has one or more eviction mills. Shop around. Talk to your peers in the property owning business. Arrange to do the preliminary work yourself. Take advantage of paralegals whenever possible. If your man/woman ever loses to a pro bono punk, move on. If you set yourself up correctly, you should win almost every time. You can easily lose at a jury trial, but you should hardly ever get there. Most judges hate to go to trial with an eviction. The only time you should end up there is a bad behavior case, and you should prepare overwhelming evidence that even a bleeding heart juror can't ignore. Testimony from third parties, especially other tenants in the building, and graphic pictures/videotape are best defense against jury nullification.

Don't skimp on maintenance

When you are searching for cash flow, it is easy to skimp on repairs. Bad move. While you are watching pennies, you need also to look at the long run. Every vacant unit should be thoroughly cleaned. Paint regularly. Replace the worn carpet. Update the appliances periodically. Spend extra money on landscaping; it is by far the cheapest source of curb appeal. Paint your building(s) regularly. Don't let them get tired looking. Maintain your systems regularly so they don't blow up and cost you big bucks. Replace the roof before it leaks. Seal the paving before the water invades and kills it. If you do all of that, you will get a better class of tenants, have less turnover, higher rents, and sell your building for a higher price when you are ready to move on.

A Few Final Words

Most small-time landlords don't raise the rents as often as they should. It is far better to raise rents regularly in small amounts than get way behind and try to get big increases. Your tenants don't have the wherewithal to handle a big increase, but they can almost always come up with a few extra bucks, especially if they shop around and find out that you are at market.

How do you find the market? The same guy (Craig of Craig's List) who is in the process of destroying the newspaper business will happily provide you with all the market information you would ever need. Just click on craigslist.com. It's even better now that everybody posts pictures. You can find comparables that exactly meet your needs. Keep your rents just slightly below the going rate, and stay current at that level. That will maximize your income and minimize your turnover troubles.

14. Office Space

I have managed a lot of office space. I owned a piece of a suburban office building for 25 years--bought at $25/foot; all cash flow was invested in tenant improvements; sold at $100/ foot--IRR never calculated due to depression that would have ensued. I have rehabbed office buildings. I've even built a few small ones (presold). Except for the presales, I have never seen any money made on an office building. The Shorenstein family in San Francisco and the Rudin family in NYC seem to have made money by buying or building in good locations and holding forever. Other than that, every office deal I've ever been around was, sooner or later, an ass kicking. The problem is turnover costs. The market gets a little soft (which it always does) and the space becomes vacant. The new tenant wants 50 or 75 or 100 dollars in tenant improvements as a condition of signing a lease. The guy down the street will say yes; so you will say yes, in order to get the deal. When I was first in the business, office space was rented absolutely "as is." Those days are gone forever, except maybe in Hong Kong and Singapore.

There is money to be made in timing deals. If you have a wad of cash (and it's always other peoples' money), you can pick up buildings for well under reproduction cost in a soft market. A little lipstick on the pig (higher occupancy, improved rents) and the passage of time (into a market of relative scarcity) will allow you to move the pig on to a greater fool at a nice mark-up. Returns are dramatically enhanced if you leverage the shit out of it, as the opportunity funds tend to do. Just be sure the pro forma in your sales brochure does not include anything resembling realistic turnover costs. The rub comes if you get the exit timing wrong and are caught will all that leverage in a soft market... with few tenants... and no buyers.

Suburban Office

One of the first rules of successful selling is to figure out who is the real buyer. I will tell you two stories to illustrate the point.

In 1957, when I was 16, I got a summer job selling used cars at the Ford dealer in Redding, CA. Mostly, I worked the "iron lot." Cars were priced from $25 to $200. We guaranteed they would run as far as the street. We took almost anything in trade. The first time I saw marijuana was a small bag offered as a down payment on one of our beauties. Occasionally, I got a chance to work the new car showroom. One Sunday afternoon (we were open "after church" on Sundays), I had the floor to myself. A couple walked in who looked like real buyers. He owned a stud mill (a sawmill turning out 2 x 4s—the standard bones of a stick built house). There were lots of little lumber mills in the Pacific Northwest before the environmentalists changed the game. The husband gravitated to a bottom-of-the-line four-door sedan. I was right on the spot with my brochure going thru the technical specifications of the car, when the sales manager called me into his office. He explained to me in no uncertain terms that I was not attending to the wife, who was looking at a Sunliner. A Sunliner was a cutting edge model that Ford had just introduced. It was a hard top convertible. The top retracted into the trunk. It was priced at least twice the number on the sedan. I explained to my boss that the husband seemed to be a very frugal fellow, not a Sunliner type. He told me, in terms that I won't repeat for these purposes, that the guy would remain celibate for a good long time if he didn't buy the Sunliner. So, I shifted the locus of my selling effort. They bought the Sunliner.

I also sold an Edsel that summer. Not many can make that claim. However, I got screwed out of the commission because the buyer was a friend of the owner.

My second customer story comes from Reno. I was running a public warehouse there in the early 70s. Public warehouses have long since disappeared. Our business was to accept merchandise for storage and charge for the handling and storage on a per-piece or per-case or per-pallet basis. It was a regulated enterprise. As a leftover from the New Deal era, we had a tariff for all kinds of goods, which regulated our charges. A true piece of regulatory insanity.

The company for whom I worked had put up a 120,000 square-foot building in Reno, because the people at the headquarters in New York thought Reno must be a big city--there was a star on the map. In fact, Reno/Sparks had a population of less than 100,000 at that time. The total population of Nevada was under 500,000, most of them in Vegas. We had some business from California, because California had an inventory tax (another bit of insanity) and the makers of cigarettes, drugs and other types of high value stuff moved it to Reno every year at tax time. However, my competitors in town had long since grabbed that business before I arrived. In terms of volume of merchandise, the biggest player in town was Sea & Ski, makers of sun tan lotion (we weren't using sunscreen in those days). They owned their own warehouse, but I thought I might be able to get some overflow. I called to get appointments; I wrote letters; I joined organizations whose membership included Sea & Ski executives. Nothing worked. I could not get in the front door. Because they were the lone big fish in a small pond, they were bombarded with sales calls, and they had learned how to insulate themselves. Finally, in frustration,

I made a cold call through a truck door on the warehouse foreman. I explained that I had a big, empty warehouse about a mile away, and access to low-priced casual labor. He asked me if I could start accepting shipments the next day. It turned out that there was a gusher of business. They sent out big shipments to retailers just before tanning season and ski season. The retailers were allowed to send back unsold items (for a refund) at the end of the season. They did so in a spectacularly unorganized fashion. The merchandise had to be sorted and repacked. My new best friend (the warehouse foreman) was happy to farm out that business. It was my first big account. I don't believe the big dogs at Sea & Ski were even aware of me or my services to them. I sent the bills to the warehouse foreman and I got paid.

The moral of these stories is that it pays to figure out, in any selling situation, the identity of the real decision maker. In the case of suburban office space, it is usually (and solely) the boss—the owner of the business, lead partner, branch manager, etc. The decision will be based, in part, on the self-image and the tastes of that decision maker. More important will be the proximity of your space to the home of that decision maker. If your competitor's building is located closer to the boss's house than yours, any quote you make will probably only be used as a club with which to beat the owner of the chosen building into submission.

The other important thing to know about suburban space is that we still have a car culture and suburbanites embrace that culture. All of the talk about transit-oriented development and lower carbon footprints are so much hogwash when it comes to owning a suburban office building. If you don't have enough parking, you will get slaughtered. Parking needs to be plentiful, be convenient and be free if you expect to lease space.

Central Business District office

Two of the best CBD office buildings in the country are the Bank of America building in San Francisco and the General Motors building in NYC. B of A is about 40 years old and GM is 50 years or more, (if recollection serves). Both command top dollar rents; stay full most of the time; and have traded at extraordinarily low cap rates.

At some stage in the cycle, money will be made on CBD buildings of the best quality, because they can hold their value over a long period of time. Why does that happen? I believe that common denominators are as follows:

1. Main & Main location. Even a few blocks off the beaten path will be deadly.

2. Classic design. Today's cutting edge architecture is tomorrow's dog.

3. Flexible floor plates and utility shafts that can serve ever-changing user needs.

4. The ability to install current technology.

If you're going to build or buy a downtown office building, I recommend that you give those criteria some serious thought.

Building Management.

I once ran a terrible little office complex of walk-up wooden buildings in a downscale suburb. I struggled to lease it. Before I arrived on the scene, two leases had been signed that took about 30% of the space—a collection agency and a credit orthodontist. Their employees and the parents of the crooked toothed kids occupied most of the parking.

A design that may not stand the test of time.

In a desperate effort to fill the space, I cut it up into smaller and smaller pieces. My smallest user was an insurance agent, who occupied 300 square feet. He bitched constantly about the temperature in his space. The zones for the HVAC were 1,000 feet, and his zone was mostly in the collection agency next door, as was the thermostat for that zone. I finally got tired of his bitching, and told my maintenance man to glue a thermostat to his wall. It gave him something to fiddle with. It worked like a charm. He played with the thermostat and quit calling me. Until the fateful day when the thermostat fell off the wall and he observed that there were no wires in evidence. If I had been anywhere close, he would have killed me. I got right on it. I told my maintenance guy, in no uncertain terms, to use stronger glue next time.

In managing office space, your issues are temperature control and elevator performance. Your constituent is the office manager and/or HR director. They are the targets of everybody's bitching, which will be passed along to you. I suggest that you pay attention to those issues, and add a few vases of flowers, and an occasional lunch, to the relationship. There is a sexist assumption in that recommendation, but my experience is that most office managers and heads of HR are women.

15. Retail

Even though my current partners and I build retail space, I know little or nothing about it. My young and energetic partner does most of the work, and we are merchant builders. We build for a national retail chain. They select the locations and provide the plans. Our value-add is navigating the entitlement process, which in dense urban locations is a lot of value to add.

Specifically, I know nothing about regional malls except that all but the A malls and B+ malls seem to be dying. I expect that a significant percentage of all the malls in the country will be dark in a few years. There are two reasons. The first is logistics. The big box retailers have very sophisticated systems; source worldwide; and operate on very thin margins. When it comes to pricing, they can clobber the department stores. The second reason is the internet. Greater selection. Better prices. No time spent looking for parking. The A malls will survive, because they are a social experience, and because they have luxury retailers as tenants. Part of the equation of luxury goods is the atmosphere of the store and the hand holding by the staff. Over the course of the last 10 years, I believe that all the net growth in retail sales is attributable to online shopping. At best, the brick and mortar retailers are treading water. Their sales volume is increasing at the rate of inflation, maybe less. There is no reason to believe this trend will end any time soon. In my view, the only reliable sectors in tomorrow's retail leasing will be ready-to-eat food, medical care, health clubs, tutoring, hair and nail care, tattoo parlors, payday lending, pawn shops, servicing of electronic devices and maybe furniture sales. You readers may be able to come up with a few more, but the list won't be long. Even palm readers will soon be on line (if they aren't already).

You Are In Business With Your Tenants

Whatever kind of real estate you own that is offered for rent, the equation is the same. The person or company that pays you rent does so because they have a use for the space. In the case of apartment dwellers, you are a partner in their paycheck. In the case of an office-building tenant, you are dependent on their sales/billings. That insight is even more applicable in retail. The location and visibility and signage and the mix of tenants in your center are vitally important to almost all tenants who would consider renting from you. There are a few who have brand power or a specialized service that will draw almost anywhere, but damn few. In general, the sales per square foot generated by a retail tenant determine the rent it can pay. As a property owner, you need to be involved in the process. You need to pick tenants who can succeed in your space. You need to be sensitive to the tenant mix. You need to help your tenants get visibility (no trees blocking the view) and signage. You need to participate in the promotion of your center. You need to keep the center looking fresh; because the shopper walking or driving by will shop based more on impulse than anything else. Even a buyer looking for a specific item in a hurry will want to get it from an attractive and convenient location. If the prospect of patronizing one of your merchants is unappealing—parking lot is dirty and full of potholes; store is hard to find; graffiti in evidence; a mugging recently reported on the local evening news—your merchants will soon go broke or move out.

A Few Warnings

In the early 90s, I ended up running some upscale neighborhood/ community centers in Houston. I inherited some third party managers and leasing agents when my organization acquired the properties. I was running a lot of industrial property in Houston, and it made sense to have me manage the retail, even in light of my profound ignorance of the property type. I knew I was in a different world the first time I went to dinner with the new vendors. My industrial managers typically took me to a barbeque joint in the ghetto for lunch or found a taco truck. Dinner was at steak houses. The women who managed and leased my retail space took me to dinner at a precious Peruvian place that had just opened and was a tough reservation. They were very proud that they had scored a table. That hadn't been a problem for barbeque. I told them in very blunt terms that I knew nothing about retail; I didn't even know how to shop; I typically read a book while my wife shopped. I told them that, within the limits of reason, I would simply follow their advice. Their first piece of advice concerned a regional credit tenant in a fairly large and ill-configured space we had who wanted out of the lease. The tenant had good credit. I had an enforceable lease. I was advised to turn them loose for a fairly modest fee, and take a new tenant the leasing agent had in her pocket. I asked to see the operation of my prospective tenant. It was two local matrons stuffed into a tiny space, who were selling tabletops (whatever the hell a tabletop is). Very little history. No credit. I swallowed hard and made the switch. One of the better moves I ever made. The merchandise was perfect for the trade area, and the owners knew half of the wealthy women in Post Oak. Business boomed and the quality of traffic it generated helped the whole center. My new tenants were able to take a very awkward configuration and turn it into a memorable shopping experience. Retailing is a thing unto itself. If you are going to build or own retail real estate, find somebody who understands the art of getting people in the door--people who want to spend money for the

Can you believe the young man from San Francisco had no idea what Tabletops are?

merchandise on offer. Those people have to find the store (visibility and signage); be motivated to enter the store (design and display); be enthusiastic about the merchandise on offer (marketing); and have the ability to buy (market research on the demographic of your trade area).

The second warning concerns the security of income stream in traditional neighborhood centers. This used to be the safest bet in the business. A grocery store on one end; a drug store on the other; some well-chosen shops in the middle; good visibility on the "go home" side of a high traffic street; good signage; and plenty of parking.

The problem is the grocer and the druggist. Most grocery chains are now selling drugs to try to increase sales per square foot, and the two drug chains that will ultimately survive (Walgreens and CVS) are mostly moving to free standing locations in dense neighborhoods. More importantly, the grocery chains may be dinosaurs. They are getting hammered by Whole Foods on the top end and by Wal-Mart/Target on the bottom. They can't compete with Whole Foods because they are union. Unions do not allow dismissal on account of poor customer service. They cannot compete with Wal-Mart because they are union. Wal-Mart is a logistics engine that wrings productivity improvements out of every sector of its business on a continual basis in order to deliver goods at a lower price. Unions are allergic to productivity gains because they threaten jobs, work rules, and tenure. Unions are profoundly reactionary. They want the procedures set in stone and left there. Work rules, job security and the perks of seniority are the hallmarks. Change is anathema. The grocery business is changing and it is leaving union shops in its dust.

My wife and I were driving up the San Diego (405) freeway in LA (a gruesome experience at almost any hour of the day). We were opposite Brentwood (former home of O. J. Simpson) when I decided that my driving skills should be enhanced by a cup of coffee. We got off the concrete monster in search of a coffee place. We found a little café a few blocks in. As we walked to the entrance of the little center in which the coffee shop was located, I said that the center would soon be bust. My wife responded that I had made an arrogant observation, since I obviously knew nothing about the center. As we entered the coffee shop, we noticed that there were for-sale signs on the fixtures. I asked the proprietor why. He said that the center had been foreclosed and he had to move. My wife asked me how I knew. I told her that it wasn't too hard. Two-story neighborhood retail doesn't work. The second story is added in order to get the pro forma to work (because too much was paid for the land and/or permits). The income from the second story gets the pro forma over the hump but that additional income never materializes in the real world.

Multi-story retail will work in really desirable locations that are so dense there is no choice except to go up. It will work of there is enough scale to create a real stream of shopper traffic to the upper stories. Mostly, it will work if the tenants on the top floor are major magnets drawing shoppers up the escalators. Other than that... death!

A related form of death is the "just off the beaten path" space. For example: space that is a few doors off the main shopping street on a side street; or space down a walkway from the main shopping street. The only way this kind of space works is with really magnetic tenants. There are a few iconic restaurants that make it. Or if you have the only appliance repair shop or shoe repair shop in town you can get away with it. Retailers who have a large following can move to a more obscure location and get away with it. Other than that, you do not want to own any retail space that is not in the heart of the action.

One of the most interesting trends in retail is brought to us by Federal Realty. They have bought free standing buildings in the fading downtown areas of upscale suburbs and moved in national tenants. The synergy has been something to behold. Federal doesn't own all of the buildings, just a significant percentage. They take advantage of existing infrastructure and traffic. Their national tenants attract more traffic, which benefits the whole area. They pick suburbs (Santa Monica, Burlingame, and Bethesda) that have lots of affluent shoppers who are logical customers for regional malls, but who would rather shop close to home, if the merchandise they want is on offer. As a result of the synergy effect, Federal is actually recreating the traditional downtown shopping experience. They have figured out that the only way to compete with the internet is to provide a social/entertainment component that the internet can't duplicate.

16. Industrial

You've Finally Hit the Jackpot

If you've read this far, you've won a literary lottery. You have arrived at the point in this tome where there will be some actual expertise on display. Although my knowledge is a bit dated (because I quit building warehouses 8 years ago), I took a street level graduate course in industrial real estate that lasted 40 years. One way or another, I've built over 40,000,000 feet of industrial space. About half of that involved soup to nuts, hands on experience. Soup to nuts refers to multi-course upscale meals that were served in an era when being overweight was a sign of prosperity, the first course being soup and the last being fruit, nuts and cheese. I have done the market research, land acquisition, entitlement, debt and equity raising, design and design review, contractor and subcontractor selection, construction management, leasing, tenant improvement design and construction management, property management, take-out funding and disposition for scores of projects ranging from 20,000 feet to over a million under one roof. In the early days, I even did some of the tenant improvement work with my own two (barely competent) hands. There are some innovations in materials handling equipment and techniques that are after my time, but I'm a genuine expert on almost every other aspect of the business. That is not an arrogant statement—it's a very straightforward business (concrete is concrete), and any damn fool can get better at something if they do it over and over (and over).

Industrial Means A Lot of Things

The list below is going to be a little arbitrary, but I will try to describe most of the kinds of structures that can be thought of as industrial real estate, and break the list into categories that make some sense. The borders are fuzzy.

Mini-storage: These units range in size from about 60 to 200 square feet. Most of the users are storing household goods that won't fit in the garage or attic. A few small businesses use them for storage, including lots of drug dealers. The first minis of which I am aware were built in Texas in the early 70s. It was a mom and pop business. As it evolved, almost all of the units are owned by large organizations, most of which are publically traded. It seems to be a decent business. It clearly requires careful and intensive management to keep the level of nefarious activity to a low roar. It seems to lend itself to volume operation/ownership. Aside from that, I know nothing.

Incubators: These units are typically 800 to 2,000 square feet. The concept was pioneered by a great Southern California developer named Don Koll. The objective was to cater to the start-up business person who was ready to make the move from the garage (to incubate). A lot of larger businesses use them as the local branch or service center or will-call center. I've built about 500,000 feet of this stuff. My observation is that the pro forma works a lot better with bigger units (more economies of scale, fewer bathrooms). Unfortunately, the users don't rent the larger units. Units of 800 to 1,200 square feet with an open office, one private office, a unisex bathroom, a laundry sink and good truck access (grade level) rent like hotcakes in a decent location. Signage that is visible to a major transit corridor helps. Good directory signage (to help the customer find the vendor once inside the complex) is a must. Tenant improvements are never appropriate. This is an industrial apartment house. You want to rent it as is.

Anyone needing alterations should pay to have them put in, and pay in advance to have them removed at the end of the lease.

Flex: This is a category that covers a very broad range. Often called office/warehouse, it usually involves a lot of interior build out. Buildings are almost always grade level, and users range in size from about 3,000 to 40,000 feet. I look at this product like office space. In many ways, it is just low-end office space. Like office space, it never seems to be worth the money required to build it (and rebuild it and rebuild it). The only way I'd consider owning it is to buy well below replacement cost. If the location has visibility; if the product has some curb appeal; if the parking is at least 3/1,000; if there is decent access to the truck doors (and maybe a little dock high loading); and if the tenant improvement process is managed carefully, you are still working hard for your money. A friend of mine says that flex land is industrial land for which you paid too much money (and office land is industrial land for which you paid WAY too much money). There is a lot of truth to that. It is a pro forma driven product.

Rear loaders: These units are typically dock-high in the 10,000 to 40,000 square foot range. The front of the building has some curb appeal, storefront and substantial parking. Office or showroom space might occupy 10-15% of the building in the front portion. The rest of the building is open industrial space served by truck doors and truck apron. The office portion needs to be parked at 4/1,000 (4 parking spots per 1,000 feet of usable space) and the remainder at 1/1,000. The truck apron should be 110 feet deep or more. Money should be spent on architectural treatment and landscaping to produce curb appeal. Lots of the tenants are sole proprietors who want to take pride in their place of business, and have some customers and/or investors calling on them. I like a clear height of 24' and lot of truck doors for maximum flexibility. These buildings get used for a lot of things—showrooms, remanufacturing, light assembly, air freight, cabinet making, etc. All of those are good uses and should be accommodated. Just be sure that your tenant improvement investments are well secured and that you have an allowance for tearing the stuff out at the end of the lease term. Aside from extra power, lighting, HVAC and restrooms, everything you put in to facilitate a lease should come out at the end of the lease term. Don't sit around with a six-fingered glove waiting for a tenant with an extra finger to fall in love with your space.

Manufacturing buildings: It is hard to describe this subclass of industrial buildings. They come in all sizes and shapes. Most are located in places that don't lend themselves to alternate use. Suffice to say this is not an appropriate category of building to develop or own. If you are being paid a fee to build it or it is presold, by all means go ahead. That is unless the source of payment is not completely reliable (and sue-able). It is OK to buy a manufacturing building if you will be entirely repaid for your efforts over the life of a lease from an AAA credit and/or you have a plan to convert the building to another use. I have gutted a few factories and turned them into multi-tenant buildings, but most factories are in locations that don't lend themselves to that plan.

Biotech (lab space): Again, a hard-to-quantify product. It comes in all shapes and sizes. Lab space is, interestingly enough, a lot more generic than it would appear at first glance. If you have space in the right location, with the right infrastructure, there is a fairly deep market. The first time I built a lab, I thought that the tenant improvements would have no useful life beyond the lease term. Much to my surprise, I was able to release very easily and almost "as is." There are a few developers in the Bay Area and Boston (maybe a few other places), and a few REITs specializing in this product, who do great business. All the rest of you should stay away from this product type, unless you are prepared to spend a lot of time and money learning the business. There is an explosion of building for the biotech sector going on in Mission Bay, an area south of downtown San Francisco that used to be a rail marshaling yard. Many of the buildings are part of the University of California medical school campus expansion, a great example of the synergy between higher education and the technology sector. I'm told that the all-in cost of the lab buildings exceeds $1,000 per square foot. That's not a pond into which you want to dip your toe, either as a builder or investor, without a great deal of due diligence.

Research and Development (R&D): This product was pioneered in Santa Clara County, California, in the 1970s. The original buildings were upscale flex structures with 5/1,000 parking. The interiors were typically a little bit of office, some training rooms, maybe a bit of prototype manufacturing, etc. There were also a lot of little "board stuffer" buildings devoted to manufacturing. As the business has evolved, manufacturing has been largely outsourced to companies like Selectron, which does nothing but contract manufacturing. They have campuses in places like Guadalajara and Singapore, upwards of 1,000,000 square feet, which accommodate some of their subcontractors, and often include housing accommodations for the work force. The original R&D buildings are mostly used as office space these days for design and marketing teams. The new social media companies prefer brick and timber funk in SOMA (San Francisco) or DUMBO (NYC). I'm not sure where the twitter types will locate once we run out of old manufacturing buildings. Some developers in San Francisco are redeveloping office buildings, and building new mid-rises to accommodate these users. It remains to be seen whether that plan will work. This is another field that requires special expertise. The people I know who have made a lot of money servicing the technology sector are very active participants in that sector. They may have made more money taking warrants in pre-IPO companies, and stock options in lieu of rent, than they made doing the real estate. In order to do that successfully, you have to acquire venture capital skills. It may be that you have to be better than the average venture capitalist, because you can't spread your bets as well as they can. You have to be right almost every time if you are providing a building to a start-up.

Warehouse: In general, these buildings may be multi-tenant (dividing to about 15,000 square feet) or single tenant (up to and including 2,000,000 square foot regional distribution centers). They are typically tilt-up concrete structures with a slab four feet above grade in order to accommodate truck loading. This product constitutes the bulk of industrial buildings in the United States. It's where all the stuff is stored that you take off the shelves of your neighborhood store every day.

In a macro sense, this is a product that is slowly dying. As the head of distribution for Dell is reputed to have said, any item you have in inventory is a mistake you made. Those are depressing words if you build warehouses for a living (which I did for 40 years). Much of the productivity growth in our economy is in the logistics sector. The ratio of goods in transit to final sales has been coming down steadily for at least the last 50 years. The general result is that the inventory of modern warehouse buildings expands at about half the rate of economic growth because, on a relative basis, it takes less warehouse space to accommodate the flow of goods. However, all of the news is not bad. A major amount of activity has shifted from retail space to warehouse space as a result of internet sales. The warehouse doubles as a store. And big box stores (Costco, Sam's, etc.) are just warehouses in retail locations. Also, the phenomena of long tails (products with a narrow but dedicated clientele) and mass customization (tailoring standard products to individual preferences) will continue to drive some demand for warehouse space.

This is certainly not a complicated product: Four walls and a roof; four feet off the ground. But there are mistakes you can make as a buyer or builder. I'll try to convey a few of them. You need to remember that everything revolves around the trailer being hauled by the truck. The trailer is eight feet across and eight feet high. The length may vary, but the other dimensions will remain the same until highway lanes are changed or all overpasses are replaced. Goods are shipped on pallets that are 4' x 4' x 4'—two high and two wide in the truck. All warehouse design needs to accommodate those immovable dimensions. A good warehouse will handle a stack of six pallets. If they are in racked storage, that means a clear height of about 28 feet. Clear height means that the top of the freight is the required distance below the sprinkler heads (usually 3'). Since freight is handled by forklifts, aisles are required to maneuver. That means that columns should be as far apart as practical on a "side to side" basis (called clear span). I prefer 60 feet (a lot of developers like 48' x 48', but I think the front-to-back 48 is a waste), so my standard design had columns on a 60' x 20' grid. Most builders build too much building on the site, because that makes for a better looking pro forma. If coverage is over 45%, watch your ass. Truck aprons need to be at least 120', and there should be additional asphalt for trailer storage. Most builders build too deep, because it is cheaper. The closer the freight is to the truck door, the more efficient the operation. My ideal depth is 200' (or 400' for a double loaded building). Obviously, a 1,000,000-foot building can't be 200' deep, but it can double load and be as shallow as possible. Next, the more truck doors, the more efficient the building. You want the truck to be as close to the place where the freight is being stored as you can get it to minimize travel time. Finally, avoid the temptation to "balance" the site by getting fill for the pad from the site of the truck aprons, thereby creating a steeply sloped truck apron. It is very hard to handle freight in and out of a trailer that sits at a slope in excess of 2%.

I've seen a lot of money wasted on buildings designed to surround state-of-the-art materials handling systems. Given a large enough volume of goods in transit and a stable enough product mix, it might make sense. However, changes in product mix and packaging and flow of goods almost always render the system obsolete before it could possibly amortize itself. Although you would be hard pressed to get anyone involved in the original decision to admit that. One thing I think I know for sure, such buildings are not good investments, unless you pro forma removal of all the specialized equipment and the remaining shell is suitable for general use. Remember that a well-designed warehouse building can have a useful life in excess of 50 years (and I've owned some buildings older than 50 years). It is highly unlikely that any materials handling system (except the pallet) has a useful life of 50 years.

17. Grab Bag

There are lots of property types we haven't covered. Hotels, regional malls, trailer parks, single family subdivisions, resorts, bowling alleys, etc. The reason for that oversight is that I have almost nothing useful to say about any of them, because I haven't built, owned or managed any of them. There are, however, a few generalities I can pass along that might be useful to you.

This is the era of virtually unlimited information. The biggest problem is not inaccessible facts; it's organizing the facts into a useful format and digesting them. If you are thinking about building or buying a new property type, there is a lot of information available about that product type. The brokers who work that product type can tell you a lot about positioning, but you should take their revenue projections with a grain of salt, and their operating expense projections with a whole 35 lb. bag of salt. There are also consultants who work most product types, some of whom are really experts. The more time and effort you spend researching a product type, the less your chances of digging a huge hole.

Second, start small. Since it's never the alligator you're looking at that bites you in the ass, you absolutely need to add some street education to your stock of knowledge. I think the biggest pitfall in the whole field of business is the mistaken assumption that success in one endeavor translates to success in another endeavor. One of my incarnations was with an organization that had done a whole lot of multi-family and industrial and a little suburban office. The big dogs decided that they needed to get into high-rise. The first one was relatively small, very well timed, and quite profitable. The next three (which came in quick succession) were a lot bigger, not nearly as well timed, and a financial dark hole. Lots of guru-quality CEOs have fallen on their faces when entering a new business.

Third, think seriously about partnering up with a veteran of the business you contemplate entering (for at least the first few deals). Find somebody with a lot of scars, maybe even somebody who had gone broke building the product you're contemplating. Failure is a great teacher; success teaches almost nothing. If you properly align incentives, you can usually find a skilled operator who is willing to teach you the business in return for a piece of the upside in your first few deals.

Finally, sell the first few deals you build. That process will teach you what is attractive to investors in the product class you're trying to master. It will also allow you to begin to differentiate between those deals that are OK, and the ones that are genuinely worth holding on to, because they will increase in value over time at a rate greater than inflation. If you are going to own a hotel forever, you want the Santa Barbara Biltmore (now a Four Seasons), not the Westin in Tustin.

18. Corporate Culture

This might seem a strange topic to use as a wrap-up for a real estate book. I think it has relevance because one of the few ways to add extra value to a real estate portfolio is astute strategy (buying or building at the right time and in the right place; selling near the top, designing for the ages) and professional execution (staying fully leased, collecting all the rent, keeping the product fresh and attractive). Well-run real estate organizations make more money than poorly run counterparts. The difference usually isn't huge, but it is not a ham sandwich.

I got my first job in 1948 as a janitor. I've worked for a lot of organizations since then. I was always a keen observer of corporate culture and behavior patterns, because the subject fascinates me. My significant organizational stints were as a junior officer in the Navy (including a year with the Marines, the most effective organization I've ever been around); as a branch manager for a national warehouse company; as a junior partner in national development organization; as Vice President in Charge of Difficult Deals at an institutional investment shop; as a founding partner of an REIT; and as a semi-active member of a small merchant building organization. The culture of each of those organizations was radically different. Those cultures evolved with turnover of personnel and the shape of the markets in which they operated. In one case, I watched an organization morph from a balls-to-the-wall development shop organized around a partnership model into a fee management shop organized around a corporate model. Much weeping and gnashing of teeth (including the legal kind) accompanied that transformation. I think the result of this grab bag of experiences is a few generalities that might be helpful to you.

The management-speak way of saying it is that you should focus on core compctence. I say you should focus on the essentials and forget most of the rest. At one point, I was in charge of a group of asset managers overseeing 50,000,000 feet of warehouse space in the Western United States. I came up with a generic "to do" list for the asset managers and their property managers, arranged in order of importance:

Lease space

Collect rent

Hustle your brokers

Be good to your customers

Know your market

Maintain your buildings

When I did my field inspections, I checked the general market occupancy. If my troops were not at least 400 basis points better than the market, harsh words were spoken. I kept a collection list with me at all times; and explained vigorously and continuously that a tenant whose rent was current was a valued customer; a tenant in arrears was a deadbeat requiring immediate eviction. I had a meal with several local brokers to see what they thought of my troops. I made visits to customers with a manager in tow to observe the body language between my manager and our customer. And I walked the buildings from top to bottom. The sight of me hauling my acrophobic butt 30 or 40 feet up a ladder created a lot of snickering, but it was worth the effort. I literally inspected vacant space with white gloves and checked to see that there was a fresh roll of toilet paper in the bathrooms. My objective was to have the best looking space, at a competitive (very competitive) price, with the simplest lease document, and an accommodating negotiator with almost complete authority to do any deal on the spot. If the deal was seven years or under, and did not involve an option to buy or a huge tenant improvement expenditure, my guy or girl could do the deal.

Whatever business you're in, respect the street. Life is not Google earth or a spreadsheet. Your business takes place on the ground and in the hearts of your customers. If you don't spend at least some time rooting around in the grubby details of your employees' daily existence, and the challenges faced by your customers, you aren't running a business; you're playing office. If you trade currencies or bonds for a living, you can spend your life behind a desk. Other than that, get out and about. Preferably walk a mile in the shoes of the people who work for you. You will be much more expert at making demands on your work force if you truly understand what you are asking them to do.

Value mistakes! Most management, as practiced, consists of a blowtorch on the ass and a fire extinguisher on the nose. The marching order is go like hell... but don't dare make a mistake. If a mistake is made by somebody trying to find a better way to get the job done, an award should be given for bravery. Clearly repeating the same mistake or acting unethically is unacceptable. Aside from that, experimentation, whether it works or not, should be valued. It is also extremely helpful, if you are the boss, to admit your own mistakes. Nobody who works for you thinks you're perfect anyway.

Most organizations have a huge amount of discord, which is terribly destructive to productivity, hidden below the surface. Most conflicts can be solved by acknowledging the issues and finding solutions with which everybody involved can live peacefully. In some cases, a termination or two may be required, but that is not usually the case. If you want openness, you are going to have to reward those with the nerve to speak up, even if you don't like what they are saying. All bosses say they value dissent and dialogue; in practice they find a myriad of ways to discourage it. Most investment committees consist of the boss (or two or three powerful people) coming to a decision, and the rest of the people in the room trying to figure out which way the wind is blowing so they can vote the right way. It's OK to value dissent and then say no as long as the rules are clear.

Personnel decisions should be binary. I can't add high enough to calculate the number of hours I've spent listening to people bitch about the inadequacy of people who work for them. That's nothing but an ego trip: Look at how valuable I am (with my finger in the dyke) and how little support I get for my heroic effort. There are only two appropriate approaches to employee relations: 100% support or termination. If an employee has the ability and willingness to get the job done, total support is in order. If either the ability or willingness is absent, termination is in order. On the morning of the termination, look yourself in the mirror and remind yourself who is at fault. Either your hiring decision or your management style (or both) was deficient. Unless you are really worried about a lawsuit, apologize to the employee for your failures, and promise to help them find a job that suits their talents.

People don't get personality transplants. You can modify behavior a little bit, usually in ways you didn't intend, but not much. The standard approach is a bonus program. It is designed by corporate social engineers to modify behavior in directions that management desires. It does modify behavior, but not in the intended fashion. Attention span beats IQ every time. Those on the receiving end of the bonus program figure out how to behave in such a way is to increase their chances of getting a bonus and maximizing the amount. The boss approves the bonus program once, the employees work all day every day at finessing it. The only successful bonus program I ever say was at an organization that existed on fee income alone (making it very easy to calculate profit). The bonus was paid at the end of each year and consisted of 25% of the company's profit. It was distributed based on the salary level of each employee (on the theory that salary levels were based on the relative value of the employee to the company and therefore the relative contribution to the production of the profit). There was virtually no way to game the system and the interests of the employee and management were almost perfectly aligned.

Positive reinforcement works better than negative reinforcement. I have worked for organizations that were fear-based, and for organizations where the basic management tool was public humiliation. Some of them are still in business, most not. The problem is that the boss cannot control every minute of every employee's time every day. Direct contact might be 1%, if that. What is going on the other 99+% of time? It's not liable to be enthusiastic production. I once worked for an organization that didn't pay its bills in a timely (or sometimes, even untimely) fashion. For a while, I worried that my reputation in the market might be ruined. Then I had a breakthrough. I told everybody I did business with that we were poor pay; that they should add 120 days of carry to their billing or barter with me. I gave rent discounts to customers who would send money to my vendors, and worked out all kinds of trades. Management's plan was to finance its business on vendor carry; the net effect was that it cost them a lot more to do business. Management was not happy about it but they put up with it because I kept the buildings full. And I was emotionally and financially prepared to be fired every day.

If you want an employee or vendor to work enthusiastically when you aren't looking, a heartfelt "thank you for a job well done" is the most powerful tool you have (but only if your body language is conveying the same message). Find some behavior you like and praise it. That will increase your chances of getting more of that behavior. Flattery is also a powerful tool. Very few human beings are immune to flattery. It costs you nothing and it yields unlimited dividends.

Thanks for noticing, boss.

Not that negative reinforcement should be completely off the table. However, it should be used sparingly. An occasional ass chewing is much more liable to generate results than a constant ass chewing. Most people can develop calluses on their butt. If you want to go at somebody, get your emotions under control; do it behind closed doors; and keep it short.

People who work for you look at what you do much more than what you say. It is useful to have a statement of corporate values and goals, but only if you are the shining example of those values and you move steadily toward those goals. If you preach cost control, and haul your family around on the corporate jet, costs will not be controlled. If you preach integrity, and cut corners, corners will be cut by most, if not all, your employees. A good leader is continuously conscious of the example he/she is setting and engages in a lot of symbolic behavior.

The End

A few years ago, we hosted a couple we've known for years for a few days at our house. During the visit, the women insisted that we go to a movie. It was the life story of a 30s composer (whose name I've repressed), who wrote a lot of very popular songs, but spent a lot of time cheating on his wife with a series of men. Due to the crowd in the theater, and the difficulty of parking, the two men and the two women sat in different parts of the theater. At the end of the movie, my friend's wife rushed up to him and said, "What was your favorite part of the movie, John?" His response was: "The End."

So, here we are at the end. I hope you got a good idea or two. If you did, my goal has been met.

About the author:

Luis Belmonte is a partner in Seven Hills Properties in San Francisco and was formerly Executive Vice President of AMB Property Corporation (NYSE: AMB). He lives in San Francisco with his wife.

Artist Scott H. Miller is a commercial real estate and environmental lawyer practicing in San Francisco.

Copies of this book can be ordered by emailing lbelmonte@7hp.com. The digital version can be purchased at Smashwords.com.